Classroom Publishing Toolbox

Creative Ways to Publish Student Writing

by

Connie S. Martin

Carson-Dellosa Publishing Company, Inc.
Greensboro, North Carolina

Credits

Editor:
Susan Morris

Layout Design:
Jon Nawrocik

Cover Design:
Peggy Jackson

Inside Illustrations:
Jenny Campbell

ISBN 1-59441-182-4

Table of Contents

Other Types of Publishing (continued)

Integrating Technology and Classroom Publishing

Celebrate Writing

Seasonal Reproducibles

Introduction

In a perfect world, students would greet each writing opportunity with gusto, seizing the chance to record their thoughts, no matter the topic. No one would ask "How many sentences do I have to write?" or "Am I done yet?" Instead, students would say things like "May we ple-e-e-ase write for just a few more minutes?"

Needless to say, most classrooms do not exist in a perfect world. Of all the things students want to do, writing is not usually high on their lists because they cannot just coast through writing. The level of difficulty varies, but at all levels, writing takes work. Writing is thinking and planning and getting thoughts on paper. It is rereading and revising and editing. It often takes more than one class period. And, it's not easy.

In order to increase the likelihood that students will develop the desire to write, we can give them authentic reasons to write and provide opportunities for them to share their writing with you, their classmates, their families, and the world. We can allow students to publish.

Years ago, publishing meant simply stapling writing papers on a bulletin board for a few days. Now, it means so much more. It certainly still includes the simple writing display, but it also includes other outlets that let students share what they want to say. Publishing can be done in many different forms, including:
- Making books
- Creating projects in which the writing is only one aspect
- Writing and performing plays
- Creating a class newspaper
- Writing and recording songs, rhymes, and riddles
- Conducting interviews
- Making posters
- Creating brochures
- Publishing on the Internet
- Holding an Authors' Tea or Writers' Fair

Classroom publishing does not have to be a huge undertaking. It can include simple, individual publishing as well as publishing of whole-class projects. A publishing center can easily be set up to allow students to self-publish when appropriate. Students at all grade levels can be taught to use the center materials respectfully, and a management system can be developed to track the center's use.

Why go to the trouble of publishing? First of all, students do not publish everything they write. Together, you decide what to publish. Secondly, publishing can be managed with relative ease. Finally, and most importantly, publishing gives value to the writing, honors the writing experience, and validates each student as an author.

A Quick Review of the Writing Process

Writing is the process of getting clear thoughts on paper in an interesting form that engages the reader. It is sharing what you want to say. A kindergartner may dictate her story to the teacher. A third grader may use the word processing program on the classroom computer and import artwork to embellish his story. Each step in the process becomes more in-depth as the writer's ability increases, but the steps included in the process remain the same.

In every classroom, the teacher adjusts instruction based on ongoing assessment of each student's abilities. Just as students in the same class read at varying ability levels, students in the same class will be writing at different levels even though they may all be writing about the same topic. There may be younger students who have an excellent grasp of expression and begin writing clear, absorbing stories at an early age. In the same class, there may be older students who are grappling with English as a new language and struggling to express themselves even in the simplest form.

There are a variety of labels to describe each step in the writing process. We will use the following:

- Brainstorming and Prewriting—the process of choosing a topic and organizing information
- Drafting—putting thoughts on paper
- Revising—selecting words to express specific ideas and putting information in a logical order to enhance understanding
- Editing—checking for correct spelling, punctuation, capitalization, and grammar
- Publishing—the sharing of writing

Reproducibles

Choosing a Topic
(page 10)

Story Map
(page 11)

Gathering Information
(page 12)

Order of Events
(page 13)

Writing Wheel
(page 14)

Revision Checklist
(page 19)

Remember to use modeling as you teach the strategies incorporated in the writing process. Students need to see you as a writer, as well, and to listen as you verbalize your thought processes while modeling each step.

Children grow as authors when exposed to a variety of writing activities. Give them opportunities to write independently as well as cooperatively. Let them try writing biographies and brochures, dialogs and diaries, fairy tales and family trees, letters and song lyrics, newspaper articles and nursery rhymes, reports and riddles, stories and speeches, and posters and plays, along with a variety of other writing activities that you and your class dream up!

Brainstorming and Prewriting

Brainstorming is the process of considering all aspects of a writing topic. Prewriting is the process of organizing information once a topic has been chosen. During brainstorming and prewriting, each student considers the purpose for writing, the format of the writing, and the audience with whom she will share her work. Are students writing poems about spring to read to parents at the next school open house? Are they writing reports about reptiles to present orally during science class? Perhaps they are writing letters to the editor of the local newspaper regarding their opinions about a district plan to require students to wear uniforms.

This first step in the writing process is crucial to student success. As young students, how many times were we given writing assignments almost as afterthoughts or as time fillers, without being given the tools and strategies to write successfully? Do you remember sitting in class, after being told to write, and not having the slightest idea of what to write or where to begin? Needless to say, you were probably not motivated to write for any other reason than to complete the assignment. We want to do better for our students.

Set students up for success. Model the thinking process that goes into choosing a topic and organizing the information to be included in the writing, then give them time to plan their own work. Students will be motivated to write and will find the next step of drafting much easier if they are writing for an authentic reason, if they have input into choosing the topics, and if they have a plan.

It is often helpful for students to have a written guide of a process to reference and to use graphic organizers to help them visualize the information they want to share as they plan.

Make a Getting Ready to Write poster to display in the classroom as a reminder of the steps in the Brainstorming/Prewriting process. Discuss each step, giving examples of purpose, format, and audience. For younger students, introduce the concepts but not the actual words *purpose*, *audience*, and *format*.

Getting Ready to Write

- I know why I am writing. (Purpose)
- I know who will read/hear what I write. (Audience)
- I know the form my writing will take. (Format)
- I have brainstormed a list of topic ideas.
- I have chosen a topic.
- I have shared my ideas with a teacher or classmate.
- I have organized my ideas and information.
- I am ready to write!

Model the use of the **Choosing a Topic** graphic organizer on page 10 to help students consider purpose, audience, and format when selecting writing topics. Display an enlarged version of the organizer on the overhead projector or on a chart. Discuss each item with students, modeling how you would complete each section when considering a writing topic.

A simple **Story Map** graphic organizer can be used to help students plan for writing fiction or for writing about specific events. (See page 11.) When writing a fictional story, the author usually creates characters that must overcome some type of problem. If a student is writing about a life event, such as spending a day at the circus, there may be no problem to be resolved, but there will be a main idea of the writing.

The **Gathering Information** graphic organizer shown on page 12 provides students with a vehicle for preparing for nonfiction writing. Have students list facts they already know about particular topics. Have students research the topics in a manner appropriate for their ability level. Students should complete the organizer by listing the new information they learned as a result of their research. Students may decide to include all or just a portion of the listed information in their writing.

Have students use the **Order of Events** graphic organizer on page 13 to decide the most important events to include in their writing (whether fiction or nonfiction) and to consider the logical order in which the events should be introduced. Some students may need to draw pictures to represent events, some may be able to list words and phrases, and others may write sentences as they plan.

The **Writing Wheel** graphic organizer on page 14 can be used to plan for fiction or nonfiction writing. The topic is listed in the center of the wheel. Words and/or phrases that represent important information about the topic are written in the spaces between the spokes. Details relating to each aspect of important information are written on the corresponding lines.

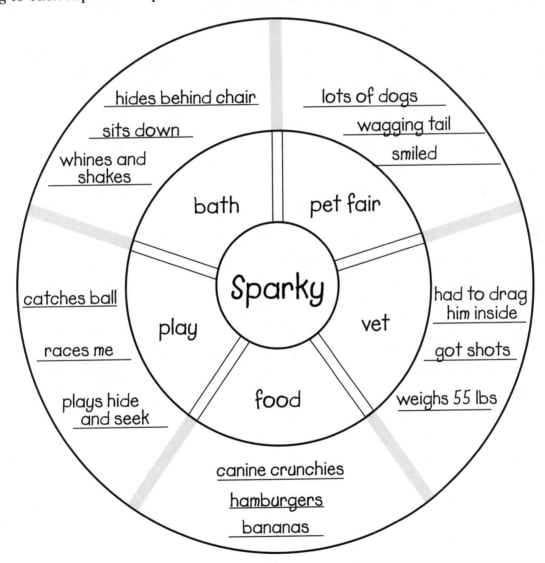

Choosing a Topic

(Purpose) I am writing to _____

_____

(Audience) My writing will be shared with _____

_____

(Format) This writing is in the form of _____

_____

I have some good ideas for writing. I could write about

_____ , or about

_____ , or about

_____

(Topic) I choose to write about _____

_____

Name _____ Date _____

Story Map

Title: _____

Who is in the story? _____

_____

Where does the story take place? _____

_____

What is the problem or main idea? _____

_____

How is the problem solved? _____

_____

How does the story end? _____

_____

Name _____ Date _____

Gathering Information

Topic: _____

Facts I know:

1. _____

2. _____

3. _____

Other:

_____

_____

Information I learned:

1. _____

2. _____

3. _____

Other:

_____

_____

Order of Events

Title: _____

First,	Next,

Then,	Finally,

Writing Wheel

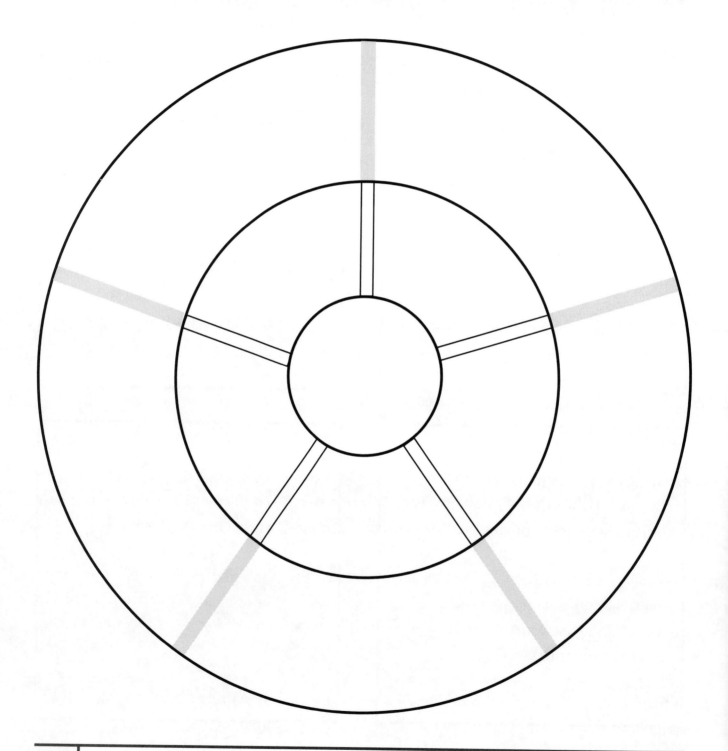

Drafting

The student has chosen a topic and organized the information to be included in the writing. Now, it is time to put pen to paper. Drafting is the process of putting thoughts on paper without regard for the rules of correct spelling, punctuation, capitalization, or grammar. It is letting ideas flow and capturing the spirit of the writing.

Although drafting may seem to be the easiest step in the writing process, it is actually quite difficult for some students. There are those who simply cannot bring themselves to put a word on paper unless they feel certain it is spelled correctly. It may take some coaxing to bring those students to the point where they can write with abandon, leaving the editing for another time. Some students feel more comfortable if they are allowed to circle any words they feel may be misspelled. The circle is a visual reminder of words they should check later when editing.

Journals

Students also become more comfortable with and more adept at drafting if they are given opportunities to write without having concerns about correctness. Journal writing can provide the vehicle for students to record their thoughts without concern for editing or for grades. Offer journal writing opportunities daily or at least several times a week. Give students a specific amount of time to write about anything they wish. The point is that they must write for the entire time, usually only five minutes or so to start with. Older students may progress to writing for 10-15 minutes at the most in one journal writing session. Less able students may simply list words or draw pictures and include words and phrases to record ideas. At all levels, students get to practice letting ideas flow and putting thoughts on paper.

You may choose to review student journals occasionally, or you may prefer to allow students their privacy; the real goal of the exercise is to give students the opportunity to practice putting thoughts on paper. You may also ask for volunteers to share their writing, giving students the option to share or to keep their writing personal.

It may be helpful to brainstorm a list of journal topics with your class. Display the list for students to consult when they have difficulty thinking of journal topics.

Simple writing journals can be prepared as often as necessary. You may choose to let students create their own monthly journals, or you may want to create a new list every month or so to keep the topics fresh and relevant to students. Add to the list as the year progresses. The list might include:

- My Best Day
- My Worst Day
- A Funny Thing Happened . . .
- The Person I Most Admire
- My Best Friend

- My Favorite (animal, food, holiday, sport, movie, book, etc.)
- What I Like Most about Me
- If I Could Have One Wish
- How I Would Change the World

During the drafting process, the writer decides if the topic will work. Is it too big to manage? Is there enough to say? Does it fit the assignment? After conferencing with the teacher or with a peer, the student may decide to change topics altogether, to refine the topic, to keep the draft in his writing portfolio for the time being and choose another piece to revise, or to move ahead to the step of revising the current writing piece.

Making a Monthly File Journal

- Insert age-appropriate writing paper into a file folder.
- Staple paper along side for Figure 1 and along the top for Figure 2.
- Cover the stapled edge with colorful cloth tape to protect against staples.
- Allow students to title the folders and decorate.
- You may choose to use a different color folder each month.

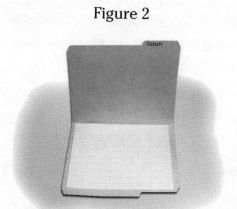

Figure 1

Folder should open from side for regular ruled paper.

Figure 2

Folder should open from bottom to top for younger students to accommodate writing paper.

Revising

Imagine you are remodeling your home. The initial structure already exists, but there are improvements you want to make. Where do you begin? A new kitchen? Changes in the bathroom? Gutting the den? The task can be overwhelming. A good way to accomplish the task is to break it into small pieces and take each piece one step at a time.

Revision is much the same for students. They have chosen topics and written about them. Now, you want more! We can make revision seem less intimidating to students by breaking down the process into individual steps and modeling strategies to reach one goal at a time. During revision, writing is assessed to be sure that:

- The topic is manageable.
- The writing has an interesting title, if appropriate.
- The introduction engages the reader.
- Relevant details support the topic.
- Information is presented in a logical or sequential order.
- Specific descriptive words are chosen to enhance the reader's understanding.
- Irrelevant details are deleted.
- The conclusion is satisfying.

Of course, each goal needs to be presented in terms young students can understand. Plan short lessons to help students assess their writing and make appropriate changes. Some self-assessing lesson suggestions are:

- Record writing topics on strips of paper. Choose topics that are obviously too broad for your students, such as animals, as well as topics that are appropriate, like favorite zoo animals. Let each student choose a strip and have the class decide if the topic is too big or just right.
- Collect and display a variety of books in your classroom. Let each student browse through the books for a few minutes, then choose one he feels has an interesting title. Have each student share the title of his chosen book and explain why that title caught his interest. Discuss titles of books not chosen and why those titles seemed dull.
- When sharing literature with children, take time to discuss the introduction. Does it make the reader want to know more? Does it hint at events to come? Does it ask a question to be answered in the course of reading?

- Show students a list of directions that explain "how to" complete a specific task, such as making a pizza or washing a dog. Write each step on a sentence strip, but place the strips in random order in a pocket chart. Discuss the steps with students and have volunteers come to the chart to place the strips in order. Discuss why the steps do not make sense unless they are written in sequential order.

- Have students close their eyes and think about the picture that comes to mind when you say a simple sentence such as, "John went to school." Replace the word *went* with more specific verbs and have students think about how the pictures in their minds change. Use verbs such as *ran, skated, skipped,* and *jogged.* Students may wish to act out each sentence. Brainstorm with students a list of overused words. Beside each word write more descriptive words. Display the list for students to reference as they write.

Example:

went: rode, hiked, jumped, skated, skipped, jogged

said: cried, yelled, whispered, asked, whined

After each activity, have students assess their own writing as it relates to the skill being targeted in the activity. Perhaps they need to choose more interesting titles or rewrite the introductions. They may need to circle the word *said* each time it is used and change each to a more descriptive verb.

After being introduced to the process of assessing their own writing with your help, students can begin to use a checklist to assess their writing before conferencing with you or a classmate. Students can use the **Revision Checklist** on page 19 to consider the state of their writing and make decisions regarding revision. It may take a student several days to review and revise a piece of writing, using the checklist as a guide.

Revision Checklist

1. The topic is not too big. ☐

2. My writing has an interesting title. ☐

3. The beginning makes the reader want to know more. ☐

4. I have written things in order. ☐

5. I have chosen words that paint a mind picture. ☐

6. Details tell about the topic. ☐

7. The ending pulls everything together. ☐

8. The best part about this writing is _____

_____

_____

9. I think I need to change _____

_____

_____

10. I have talked about my writing with _____

Editing

Editing is the process of checking a revised piece of writing for correct spelling, punctuation, capitalization, and grammar. Depending on the ages and ability levels of your students, you may wish to have them edit writing for only one item at a time. Plan short lessons to review specific rules regarding each area, then have students assess writing only in regard to that particular skill. Students should confer with you and/or classmates in order to be certain the writing has been correctly edited. Not all pieces of writing will make it to the editing stage. At any given time, a student will probably have several pieces of writing in her writing portfolio. Whenever possible, allow the student to choose the writing she wishes to revise and edit.

Create an Editing Checklist similar to the one below. The checklist is presented in general terms and should be adapted to each student's ability level. For example, younger students may only know to capitalize the beginning of each sentence, while older students should know to capitalize holidays, names, etc. The checklist should serve as a guideline for students to review before conferring with you.

Editing Checklist:
- Capital letters are in the right places.
- Words are spelled correctly.
- I have used correct punctuation marks.
- I have double-checked my grammar.
- I am ready to publish!

Once a student has progressed through the prewriting, drafting, revising, and editing stages of the writing process, he has reason to celebrate! It is time to share his writing with the world . . . or at least with classmates. This writer is ready to publish.

Setting Up a Classroom Publishing Center

Students have finished their writing. Every "t" is crossed and every "i" dotted. The only decision to be made is how to share the writing. How do we publish? Remember, the act of publishing can be very simple or quite elaborate. Students may publish writing independently, in cooperative groups, or as whole-class projects. The depth of involvement depends on the writing project. Students will usually be working on different steps in the writing process at any given time. Even if students are working on a whole-class project, some will complete their tasks and be ready to publish before others. How can all of this be managed? Simple— you can set up a publishing center in your classroom. Even very young students can learn to publish in an orderly manner if you model the procedure and provide directions for use and opportunities for practice. In order to know which students are ready to come to the publishing center, use a pocket chart to keep track of students' progress as they move through the steps in the writing process.

Write each stage of the writing process on a sentence strip and place it at the beginning of a row in the pocket chart. Write each student's name on an index card. Have each student place her card on the row beside the name of the stage she is working on. Students should move their cards each time they progress to a new stage. With a quick glance, you can see which students are ready to publish.

Reproducible

Parent Letter
(Page 25)

Your publishing center will be ever-changing as you become more comfortable with the process. Feel free to start small; a publishing center can simply be the area where students come for materials to staple their writing to pieces of colorful construction paper for display. On the other hand, the publishing center might include all types of materials for creating and decorating original books. It may include blank audiotapes for recording original stories. There may be disposable cameras to use to provide pictures to accompany special writing projects. The center may be stationed near classroom computers so that students can use software to publish. Some may publish on the classroom Web site on the Internet.

Materials and Supplies

There are already many materials in your classroom that can be gathered for use in setting up a publishing center. Students would come to the center with their completed and corrected writing in hand. Think of the supplies students would need to encase and decorate their writing in some type of simple cover.

1. For each student, precut two sheets of colorful construction paper to cover the size of students' writing paper and slip the writing page or pages between the construction paper.
2. Staple along one edge and cover the stapled area, front and back, with colorful cloth tape to cover sharp stapled edges.
3. Let students use a variety of materials to display the titles and their names as the authors.
4. Have students decorate the covers.

A simple center like this might have the following supplies:

- Selection of colorful construction paper
- Colorful pencils
- Crayons
- Markers
- Letter stamps
- Stamp pads
- Stapler
- Cloth tape in a variety of colors
- Scissors

This center could easily be expanded with the addition of materials such as:

- Gel pens
- Glitter pens
- Seasonal stamps with colorful stamp pads
- Scissors that cut decorative designs (for trimming edges)
- Decorative stickers
- Letter stencils
- Design stencils

Management

As always, young students require adult supervision. An assistant or parent volunteer may be able to oversee the use of the publishing center. If no help is available, you may oversee small groups of students at the publishing center while other students are involved in independent activities.

At all age levels, students need to know where to find and return materials and how to use them properly. They also need to know where to put the finished products. Teach a short lesson on using the publishing center. Explain where all materials are stored. Demonstrate the proper use of each.

Publishing Center Rules

1. Collect materials and supplies for your project.
2. Follow project directions.
3. Uncap one marker at a time.
4. Just a little glue will do.
5. Return supplies.
6. Clean up.
7. Put your completed project in the basket.

If possible, create a chart that lists your rules for using the publishing center. Display the rules at the center and review them as needed. For younger students, include an illustration with each rule to act as a visual reminder.

Sample Lesson: Using the Publishing Center

Show students a copy of a book that is a class favorite. Begin by saying, "The author wrote this book to share what he or she wanted to say to others. When writing is shared, it is published. Writing does not have to be in a book in the library in order to be published. The writing we do in the classroom is published when we share it with others. We may share it with a friend, with the class, with the whole school, or with the entire world! When we publish, we want to make our writing look special. You may want to write the title on the cover of a book you have written by using letter stamps and glitter pens. Or, you may wish to decorate your cover with stickers or drawings."

Tell students that there will be a special place in your classroom to take writing to be prepared for publishing. Gather students around your publishing center. Explain how students will know when they may come to the center and who will be supervising their time spent in the center. Show students where materials will be located. Display your rule chart and go over each rule. Answer any questions students may have. Ask for a volunteer to read each rule again. Choose students to demonstrate proper use of materials. Let students know when the center will be open for use.

The depth and breadth of the materials in your center will depend on your comfort level, your materials budget, and the willingness of parents and volunteers to provide some additional materials and assistance. Send a letter to families explaining what a publishing center is and why it is important. Use the letter on page 25 or create one that better reflects the needs of your class. Ask parents to provide materials from an enclosed list in lieu of teacher gifts during the year. You may also ask families to donate more expensive items, such as blank cassettes or disposable cameras in honor of their children's birthdays.

Your publishing center may be simple or ample. The point is to publish. The remainder of this book is filled with specific ideas and plans for publishing everything from books to brochures. Choose one you like and just get started!

Dear Parents or Guardians,

Your child will become a published author this year! We will do lots of different writing projects in our class as we learn to share what we want to say. When we share our writing with others, we "publish" that writing. Some projects will be simple while others may be more complex. Your child will bring home original books he or she has written. We may even attempt to make a video of a play we write and perform as a class.

There will be a Publishing Center in our classroom where students can prepare their individual writing projects for publication. We will need a wide variety of supplies to stock our center. The school provides the basics like construction paper, glue, and scissors, but we would like to encourage creativity by stocking our center with everything from colorful pencils to crepe paper. Please consider donating one or more of the following items for our center. We ask you to donate items from the list instead of sending teacher gifts during the year. The greatest gift we can receive is help in providing the best education possible for your child. You may also consider sending items in honor of your child's birthday instead of sending food.

Requested items for our Publishing Center:

- Colorful pencils
- Gel pens
- Glitter pens
- Letter stamps
- Seasonal shape stamps
- Washable stamp pads (variety of colors)

- Washable markers
- Cloth tape in a variety of colors
- Scissors with decorative edges for cutting
- Letter stencils
- Design stencils
- Decorative stickers

Other special items:

_____

Thank you for your support. We know you will enjoy sharing the experiences ahead as your child grows as an author and publishes many pieces this year.

Sincerely,

Making Books

At a Chinese restaurant, you might choose one item from column A, one from column B, and one from column C to create your individual order. There is an almost limitless number of variations from which to choose. Making a book is much the same. In most cases you must choose the kind of paper for the text, the type of binding that will hold the book together, and the cover that will encase it all. The number of possible combinations may not be limitless, but they certainly are numerous. Here are some basics to help you choose, but feel free to change things to suit your needs.

Paper

To some extent, the type of paper used in a book will depend upon the age and ability levels of your students, as well as any school policy related to the type of writing paper students are required to use at each grade level. You may have students who really need lined paper to help them write legibly. You will probably also have students who can write in a reasonably straight line on blank paper. There may even be times when it really doesn't matter whether the writing line is straight! You may wish to have students cut around the text and paste the text to colorful construction paper. If students type their writing into a computer word processing program, they have the opportunity to choose the size of the type, variety of lettering styles, and possibly, the color of their printed text. They may have the option to choose from among colorful printer papers with a variety of borders.

Visit a craft or paper specialty store and purchase a few sheets of specialty paper for the students to look at and feel. Let them notice the different textures, colors, and fibers. If you find yourself feeling adventurous, demonstrate how paper is made! There are a variety of Web sites that have simple instructions for making paper.

A variety of stationery patterns are provided at the end of this book. Students can use the stationery to write about holidays, seasons, or special events. Teach students about friendly letters and how correspondence between friends and family used to take place primarily using pen and paper.

Covers

Place a blank sheet of paper or construction paper at the beginning and end of each book. Allow each student to decorate the front sheet as she wishes. Be sure to have her include the title and author on the front sheet.

A more permanent and decorative cover can be created using a modified file folder and wrapping paper, cloth, or wallpaper samples in the following manner:

Making a Simple Book with a Cover

1. Fold 8 ½" x 11" (21.5 cm x 28 cm) sheets of white paper in half to create the pages of your book.
2. Cut an additional sheet of 8 ½" x 11" (21.5 cm x 28 cm) paper in half.
3. Trim a file folder to be 1" (2.5 cm) wider than the folded pages along all edges.
4. Staple the writing pages to the file folder along the center fold. Most staplers swing open to allow you to staple longer items. Place the book on a soft surface, such as corkboard, to allow staples to penetrate the folder.
5. Cut a piece of decorative wrapping paper, wallpaper sample, or cloth to be 1" (2.5 cm) wider than the file folder along all edges.
6. Fold the paper along the top and bottom edges, cutting a slit in the paper where the folder creases in the center. Glue the paper to the file folder.
7. Fold the paper over each side of the folder, trimming the corners as shown.
8. Glue one piece of the halved paper to each inside cover to hide the edges of the wrapping paper.

Bindings

The pages of a book must be physically connected in some way. The simplest way is to staple sheets together. However, there may be times when you prefer to use other methods such as:

- Punch holes along the left side or top of the book and tie with yarn or ribbon, or secure with rings or brass fasteners.
- Use binding combs and a bookbinding machine. Some schools or school districts have bookbinding machines teachers may use upon request.
- Stitch the binding:

  1. Take two pieces of poster board cut to the same size as the writing paper. With a pencil, mark small dots along the left edge of one piece of poster board about ½" (1.3 cm) from the edge and about 1" (2.5 cm) apart.
  2. Place the writing paper between the two pieces of poster board. Be sure the marked board is on top. Place paper clips around the edge of each unmarked side to keep papers in place.

  3. Place the stack on a protected surface, like an old magazine or a piece of corkboard. Use a large needle, nail, pushpin, or other pointed object to poke through each marked dot. Be sure the hole passes through each layer. Reduce the chance of tearing the paper while sewing by placing a paper hole reinforcement over each hole.
  4. Thread a large needle with embroidery thread. Remember to put a knot in the end. Place the tip of the needle under the stack. Come up from underneath, poking a hole through the first marked dot. Come around the marked edge, placing the needle underneath again, and come up through the next marked dot. Continue stitching to the end.
  5. Stitch again in the opposite direction to reinforce the binding.
  6. Knot the ends together and tuck them behind the stitches.

Folded Paper Books

Create a four-page blank book that requires no special binding by simply folding one sheet of paper. Just remember, the smaller the paper you begin with, the smaller the final book.

1. Fold a sheet of paper in half side-to-side two times.
2. Unfold the paper once and refold it in half top-to-bottom.
3. Open the paper and cut a slit from the center of the folded edge to the middle of the paper.
4. Fold top to bottom.
5. Fold in half side-to-side to create the four-page book.

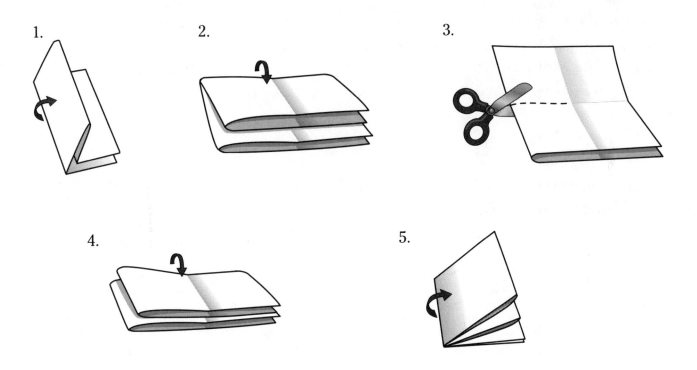

Suggested Activities:

Keep lots of these blank books on hand, ready to use. During blocks of downtime, have students make blank books.

- Have students write the letter of the week on each page and draw an object that begins with the corresponding letter.
- Have students write a simple word on each page and illustrate the meaning of the word.
  Example: (opposites) happy/sad; hot/cold; smiley face/sad face; sun/snow
- Have students copy a simple sentence and complete it on each page.
  Example: I like to eat _____ .
  Let students include illustrations. Encourage volunteers to share their books with the class. Let students take the books home to share with parents.
- Students can write about and illustrate four things they learned about a certain topic in class.
- Have students write the steps and illustrate the process for solving math problems.
- Let students interview family members or friends and write a least one interesting fact on each page.

Shape Books

Shape books are such fun! Consider a basic shape related to a theme or unit of study. Be sure the shape can be drawn in a "boxy" manner that allows for a good amount of writing space. For example, with a story about "Winter Fun," the mitten shape provides much more writing space on each page than glove shape does.

The glove shape has a small amount of writing area.

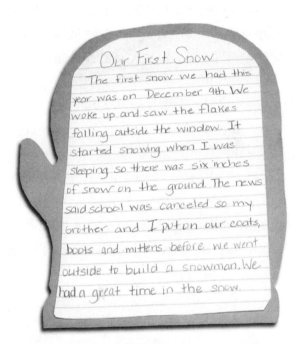

The mitten shape has more writing area due to its "boxy" shape.

Patterns are provided for a variety of themes on the following pages, but you may want to be creative and design your own shapes. Use the patterns to cut the writing paper and cover to the same size and shape. Students will enjoy sharing their shape books while turning the oddly shaped pages.

Remember to show students an example of a completed shape book before asking them to attempt the process. Shape books make decorating a bulletin board easy and give the published writing a three-dimensional feel. The possibilities are endless!

Making Shape Books

1. Create a template of the desired shape. (Several patterns have been provided on the following pages. Each pattern should be enlarged 200% on your copier to create an 8.5" x 11" (21.5 cm x 28 cm) pattern.)
2. Cut writing paper and front and back cover sheets using the template as a guide.
3. Bind pages as desired.
4. Have students write final copy on blank pages or cut and paste writing to blank pages. Let them illustrate the final copy.
5. Tell students to write the titles and authors, then decorate the covers.

Suggested Activities:

These Suggested Activities: for younger students provide opportunities for working with vocabulary, completing sentences, and/or reading and following directions. Students need to develop a strong reading vocabulary if they will become strong writers. Some activities require teacher-prepared books for students to complete. Write the necessary text on each page and make copies before combining pages to create the prepared books. You may choose to share and discuss books or stories related to the writing theme before having students create their own books.

Example of open Pumpkin Book

Apple

- Have students draw and label or cut out, paste, and label pictures of fruit. Let them practice oral communication by telling about their books.

- Prepare apple books ahead of time. Include 10 pages per book. On each page, write a sentence to tell students how many apples to draw. ***Example:*** *I can make 1 apple. I can make 2 apples. etc.* Have students read their books to their families.

- Take a field trip to an apple orchard. Have students write about the outing.

- Let students make applesauce. Have students write and illustrate each step. (Before completing any food activity, ask parental permission and inquire about students' food allergies and religious or other food preferences.)

- Study the growth cycle of apples. Have students write about the growing process.

- Share the story of Johnny Appleseed. Have students research the life of John Chapman and write about the events they found most interesting.

- Have students write stories based on the following prompt: *Once, I found an apple made of gold . . .*

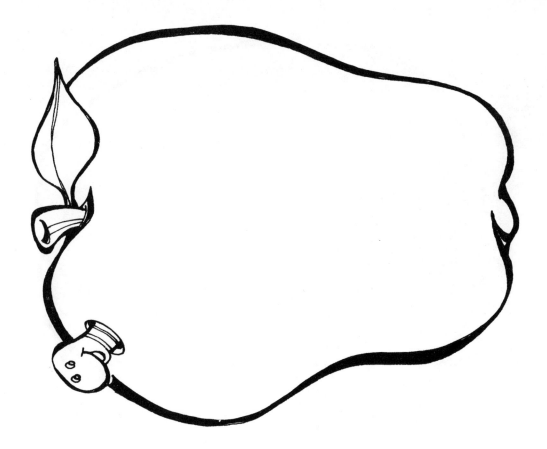

Pumpkin

Many of the ideas suggested for the apple book can also be used with the pumpkin template. Additional suggestions are as follows:

- Have students draw or cut, paste, and label pictures of objects that begin with the letter "*p.*"
- Let students roast pumpkin seeds and describe the process.
- Have students write the steps for carving a jack-o'-lantern.
- Have students visit a pumpkin patch and write about their trip.
- Read *Too Many Pumpkins* by Linda White (Holiday House, 1997). Have students list how many different ways pumpkins can be prepared as a meal.
- Read *The Pumpkin Book* by Gail Gibbons (Holiday House, 2000). Have students write the stages a pumpkin goes through from planting to harvest.
- Story prompt: *I was scooping the seeds out of my pumpkin when I found something strange hidden inside . . .*

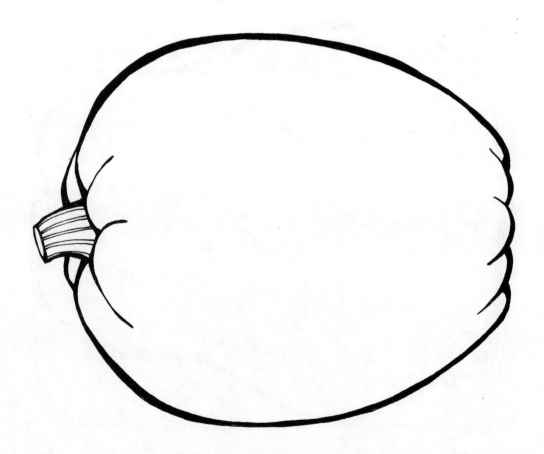

Mug of Hot Chocolate

- Have students write words that have the short /o/ vowel sound as in *hot* and the first *o* in *chocolate*. Encourage students to illustrate the meanings of as many words as possible.

- Prepare books ahead of time. Include as many pages as you wish. On each page, write the following: *Who has my hot chocolate?* _____ *has my hot chocolate.* Let students fill in the blank on each page to make silly sentences. (*The octopus has my hot chocolate.*) Ask students to include an appropriate illustration for each page.

- Make hot chocolate for everyone! Have students write the steps in the process. (Before completing any food activity, ask families' permission and inquire about students' food allergies and religious or other preferences.)

- Read the story *Lucky Pennies and Hot Chocolate* by Carol Diggory Shields (Dutton Books, 2000). Have students write about things they have in common with people they love.

- Story prompt: *As I leaned in to take a sip of my hot chocolate, a genie suddenly appeared in the steam . . .*

Snowman

- Prepare books ahead of time with this sentence on each page: _____ *is cold.* Have students fill in the blank on each page to identify something cold.
- Make a class book entitled "Snowy Day Fun." Have each student complete the following sentence and identify the page as her own: *On a snowy day, I like to _____ . (Suzie)* Have students include illustrations. Combine all pages to create a class book.
- Have students write and illustrate the steps for making a snowman.
- Read *Martin Macgregor's Snowman* by Lisa Broadie Cook (Walker & Company, 2003). Have students write about things they would do if school was canceled because of snow.
- Have students write cinquain poems about a snowman.
  Line 1: Write a noun.
  Line 2: Write two adjectives describing the noun on Line 1.
  Line 3: Write three words ending with *-ing* (action words) that describe what the noun on Line 1 might do.
  Line 4: Write a phrase describing the noun on Line 1.
  Line 5: Write a synonym of the word on Line 1.
- Story prompt: *My snowman came to life!*

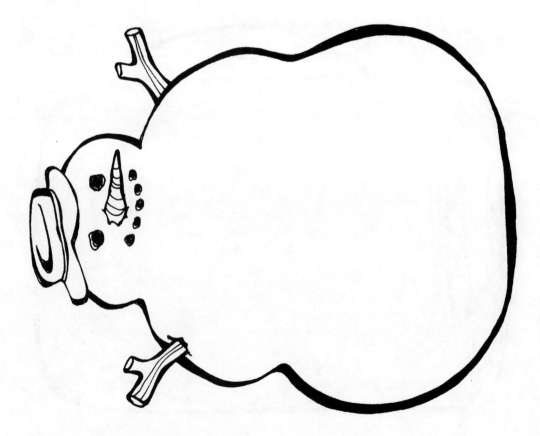

Easter Egg

- Have students write words that have the short /e/ vowel sound as in *egg*.
- Prepare books ahead of time. Write one direction on each page. Have students read and follow the direction.

  Example(s): Draw an egg with red and green dots. Draw one blue egg and one red egg.

- Dye eggs! Have students describe and illustrate the steps in the process.
- Read *Eggbert: The Slightly Cracked Egg* by Tom Ross (Putnam Publishing Group, 1997). Have students write about the other items in the world that are cracked.
- Read *Chickens Aren't the Only Ones: World of Nature Series* by Ruth Heller (Putnam Publishing Group, 1999). Have students write about and draw pictures of animals that lay eggs.
- Story prompt: *I found a rainbow colored egg under a bush. I cracked it open and discovered . . .*

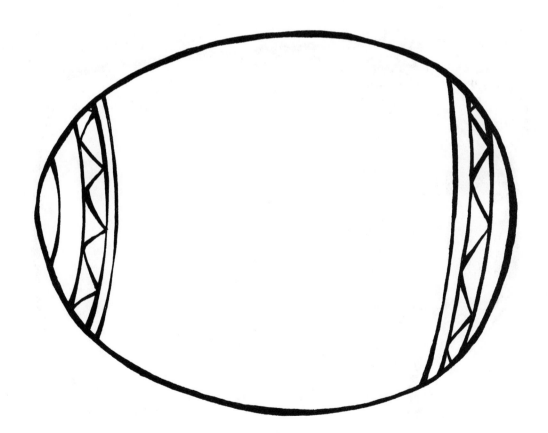

Sand Bucket

- Have students write and illustrate the meanings of words that rhyme with *sand*.

- Prepare books ahead of time. Include a page for each day of the week. On the first page, write *On Monday, I found a _____ in the sand.* On the next page, write *On Tuesday, I found a _____ in the sand.* Continue with a different day of the week on each page. Have students fill in each blank as they wish and illustrate each page.

- Have students write about favorite beach vacations, or about any special days spent playing in sand.

- Read *Super Sand Castle Saturday* by Stuart J. Murphy (HarperTrophy, 1999). Have students list some items in the classroom that could be used for nonstandard measurement. Then, have students explain why we use rulers and metersticks to measure.

- Have students research what animals live in the sand. Then, have them write about what they found in their research.

- Story prompt: *I dug my way to China!*

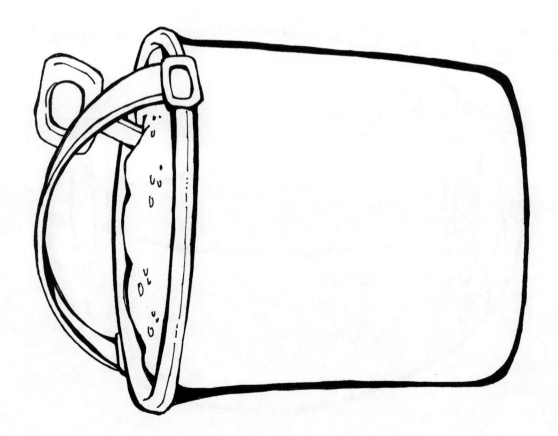

Beach Ball

- Make a word/picture book for the letter *b*.
- Brainstorm a list of beach activities with students. Share a book about going to the beach. Prepare writing books ahead of time. Write the following sentence on each page: *We can _____ at the beach.* Repeat on as many pages as desired. Have students fill in the blank on each page with an activity they could do at the beach. Let students illustrate each page.
- Have students write about the best (or worst) times they have had at the beach or on any vacation.
- Have students write lists of things they would need if they were going on vacation to the beach.
- Have students write all of the directions needed to blow up a beach ball. Make sure they include all of the important details, such as opening the spout at the beginning and quickly closing the spout at the end.
- Story prompt: *I was sitting on the beach, when suddenly I saw something strange in the water . . .*

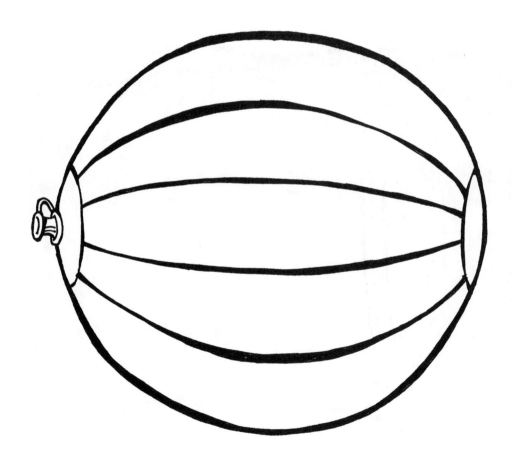

Flag

- Make a word/picture book for words that begin with the blend *fl*.

- Have each student complete and illustrate the sentence: *I love my country because* _____. *(Juan)* Combine pages into a class book.

- Have someone show students how to correctly fold a country flag. Have students write about the process.

- Give students an opportunity to research the history of the country flag and write at least five facts they have learned.

- Have students design flags for "new" countries. Have them describe the new countries (location, weather, laws, population, etc.) on the pages inside the book.

- Have students brainstorm and list different types of flags and places you might see them. (State and national flags, flags at racing events, decorative flags, maritime flags, team flags, marching band flags, etc.)

- Writing prompt: Write about being a good citizen. What does it mean to you?

Picture Frame

- Prepare books ahead of time for students to complete. Write each of the following sentences on a separate page: *My name is _____ . I am _____ years old. I have _____ hair. I have _____ eyes. I like to _____ .*
- Prepare books ahead of time for students to complete. On each page, write the following sentence: *I like myself because _____.* Have students state a different reason on each page.
- Have students draw pictures of their families on the covers and write about each family member.
- Have students choose their favorite drawings by famous artists. Lets students recreate the pictures in the frame provided. Then, have students write some facts about the artists on the pages inside.
- Story prompt: *I woke up this morning as usual, but everything was crazy! My family has gone nuts! First of all . . .*

Treasure Chest

- Prepare books ahead of time for students to complete. Have students fill in the blank on each page to complete the following sentence: *I found a _____ in the treasure chest.*

- Have students research the history of famous pirates and write about the ones they found to be most interesting.

- Have students research the subject of the country's currency. How is it made? Who decides how each denomination looks? What happens to old money?

- Have students write about things they treasure.

- Story prompt: *When I went into the attic of the old house, I found a chest covered in dust. I slowly opened the lid and . . .*

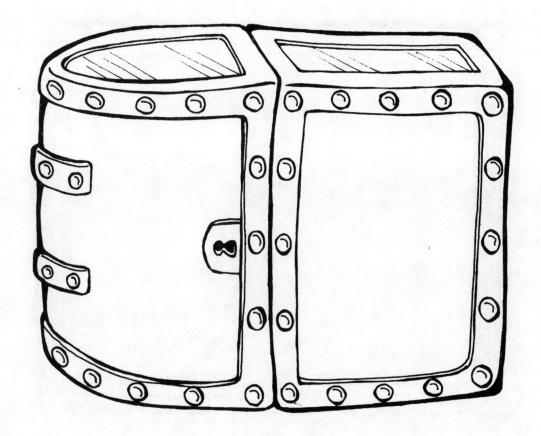

Book

- Have each student complete the following sentence: *I like books about* _____ . *(Anna)* Let students illustrate the sentences. Combine pages to create a class book.
- Have students write about their favorite authors.
- Ask students to write a book report.
- Have students write "Books I Read in _____ Grade" on the covers of the books. Throughout the year, students can write the titles and authors of books they read independently.
- Have each student contribute a page with an age-appropriate joke. Compile the jokes into a class book. Brainstorm with students to come up with a fun title.
- Have students bring in favorite family recipes. Compile into a class book. Make enough copies of the compiled book for each student to have a copy.
- Story prompt: *It looked like an ordinary book, but when I opened it, I was sucked inside!*

Envelope Books

Making an Envelope Book

1. Cut a piece of stiff construction paper to the desired size for each writing page as well as for the front cover and back cover.
2. Bind pages as desired.
3. Attach an envelope with glue or double-sided tape to the bottom of each page as shown.
4. Complete writing activity on each page.
5. Place related items in the corresponding envelopes.

Suggested Activities:

- Let each student make a yearlong memory book. Each time students take a field trip, have a special class visitor, etc., have them dictate or write about the occasion at the top of a page. You may want to take pictures and allow each student to put a picture in the envelope at the bottom of the page. Or, let students illustrate the event to put in the envelopes. Students may collect mementos, such as tickets or programs, or flowers or leaves, to put inside the envelopes. Collect books after each writing entry and store during the year, returning them to students for each new writing occasion. Send the books home at the end of the year.

- Practice choosing specific descriptive words by creating riddle books. Have each student write a description of a mystery object at the top of a page. Have her draw a picture of the object to insert in the envelope. During the next few days, let students share their riddles while classmates try to guess the answers. ***Example:*** *I am always white. I am frosty cold. Sometimes I wear a tall, black hat. My nose might be a pointy carrot. I melt in the sun. What am I? (snowman)*

Pocket Books

Make books with pockets instead of envelopes. Use the same procedure as for envelope books, substituting half-page pieces of construction paper trimmed with decorative scissors for the envelope on each page. Make sure to use glue only on the sides and bottom of the half page.

Flip Books

Making a Flip Book

1. Cut a piece of construction paper to the desired size for each writing page as well as for the front and back covers.
2. Cut a smaller piece of construction paper to attach to each writing page.
3. Use glue or double-sided tape to attach the top of the smaller piece of paper to the top of each writing page.
4. Bind as desired.

Suggested Activities:

- Have younger students make a book of opposites. Have them write words on the pages, and their opposites under the flip sheets. Exchange books and enjoy!
- Make riddle books or joke books.
- Have students consider a current unit of study. Have them write an incomplete sentence on each page and write the answer under the flip sheet. Older students may use a multiple-choice format. Let students exchange books to see how much they know!

Accordion Books

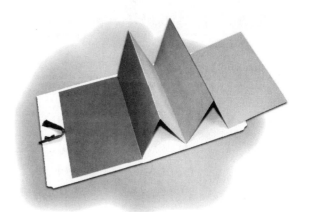

Making an Accordion Book

1. Choose the number of desired pieces of 8½" x 11" (21.5 cm x 28 cm) construction paper. Choose a light color of paper if students will write directly on the construction paper. One piece will equal four writing pages, if front and back are used.

2. Connect pieces of construction paper end to end with glue, rubber cement, or two-sided tape to create one long sheet.

3. Fold the first sheet in half by folding the left edge toward the right edge.

4. Hold the folded piece in your hand and fold the next sheet to the back.

5. Continue folding, accordion style.

6. Trim a file folder to be 1" (2.5 cm) wider than the folded sheets.

7. Glue the last sheet to the folder as shown.

8. Punch a hole in the center of the edge of the folder.

9. Pull a piece of ribbon or yarn through each hole, knotting the end on the inside cover.

10. Tie the ribbon or yarn to hold the book closed.

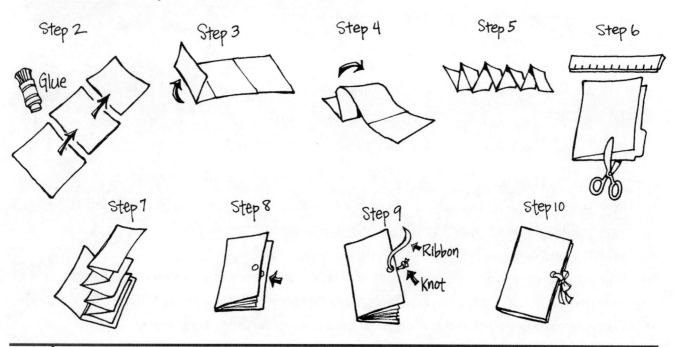

Step 2 — Glue Step 3 Step 4 Step 5 Step 6

Step 7 Step 8 Step 9 — Ribbon, Knot Step 10

Suggested Activities:

Write about things that occur on a time line or have a specific process. Have students write and illustrate:

- the days of the week and special things they do on each day
- the months of the year and special events that occur each month
- the steps in a process, such as the life cycle of a chick, the water cycle, or how a seed becomes a plant
- their daily observations of the progress of a science project
- the major events in the life of a person being studied
- an autobiography
- a fiction story
- a series of cause/effect events

Tab Books

When writing about a process of five steps or less, make Tab Books. Inexpensive self-stick tabs that can be written on are available at most office supply stores. You will need four or more tabs per book. Some tabs come in a variety of colors. A green tab could designate the first step in a process, blue tabs might designate additional steps, a yellow tab could indicate the beginning of closure, and a red tab might signal the final step.

Making a Tab Book

1. Stack together three sheets of 8½" x 11" (21.5 cm x 28 cm) white paper.
2. Turn paper to landscape view, then fold in half left-to-right.
3. Fold an 8½" x 11" (21.5 cm x 28 cm) sheet of construction paper and place around white sheets to form front and back covers.
4. Open the book to the center and staple along the center fold.
5. The first white sheet will be the title page.
6. Open the book to the first double-page spread.
7. Place a self-stick index tab at the top left edge of the sheet.
8. Write the word *First* on the tab.
9. Turn to the second double-page spread. Place tab labeled *Next* as shown.
10. Continue to label each double-page spread as needed.

Suggested Activities:

- Have students illustrate and write the steps in a process, such as how they get ready for school or how to make an ice cream sundae.
- Have students write about the important events in the life of a person they are studying.
- Let students write about the sequence of events in a time period that the class is studying in social studies.
- Ask students to write about the steps in a science experiment.

Clever Container Writing

What exactly is "container" writing? It is writing that is contained in some sort of packaging. The packaging may or may not include objects related to the writing text. Students may go on a field trip and acquire mementos of their experience. When they return to class, they can write about the field trip and include the mementos in the writing packages. A writing package may be a file folder, a manila envelope, a paper bag, a bakery box, a resealable plastic bag, a photo sleeve, or any number of containers you might consider. Remember, some students may need to dictate what they want to share, while others will write, and write, and write! A few ideas are shared here to get you started. Remember, any of these ideas can be mixed and matched regarding materials used and lessons targeted. It's all up to your discretion! Also, plan ahead and ask parents to donate items needed to create the projects you want to try. Most of the items can be purchased inexpensively at local paper, hobby, or party stores.

Be sure to let students regularly share their writing with others. You may choose a few students each day to share a piece of published writing. Or, pair students and give each student an opportunity to share with his partner. Perhaps a volunteer could listen to several students at each visit. You may have students take the writing home to share with families.

Published writing might be displayed in the writing center. Or, it may be displayed in the reading center where students can read the pieces on display each time they visit that center. Find a way that works for you and your students. Just publish!

Reproducibles

Book Review
(page 57)

New Ending
(page 58)

Characters
(pages 59-60)

Settings
(pages 61-62)

Conflicts (Problems)
and Situations
(pages 63-64)

Days of the Week
(page 67)

Pockets

A writing pocket can be any size. Just make it about 1" (2.5 cm) wider than the writing paper to ensure the paper will fit inside the pocket. A writing pocket can be made out of any material that is strong enough to hold the writing paper. Use staples, glue, or double-sided tape to secure the sides and bottom pieces of the pocket to each other, leaving the top edge open to receive the writing paper. If desired, writing pockets can be attached to a bulletin board for display with staples or thumbtacks.

Construction Paper Pocket

Make a writing bulletin board that can remain unchanged for long periods of time that includes a writing pocket for each child. Students may exchange the pieces of writing displayed in their pocket over time, but the pockets can remain the same. Prepare the pockets ahead of time for students to decorate or have students make and decorate their own pockets, depending on ability level.

Making Writing Pockets

1. Attach two 9" x 13" (23 cm x 33 cm) pieces of colorful construction paper on three sides.
2. Have students title the pockets "My Writing Pocket."
3. Let students decorate their pockets. Be sure their names are displayed on the fronts of the pockets.

Suggested Activities:

- Incorporate writing activities with as many units of study as possible.
- Change the writing frequently. Allow students time to read the writing of other students.
- Display a story prompt on a bulletin board along with the writing responding to the prompt.
- Have each student write two to three positive comments about each piece she reads and share the comments with the author.

Felt Pockets

Create new writing pockets each season. Use colors that represent the season.

Making Felt Pockets

1. Attach two 9" x 13" (23 cm x 33 cm) pieces of colorful felt on three sides.
2. Have students use decorative stickers to embellish the fronts of the pockets.
3. Display as desired.

Suggested Activities for Fall:

* Read *Time to Sleep* by Denise Fleming (Henry Holt and Company, 1997).
  Writing prompt: Tell how Bear might wake up each animal friend in spring.
* Have students research the topic of hibernation.
* Read *Fall is Here! I Love It!* by Elaine W. Good (Good Books, 1990).
  Writing prompt: Tell about the _____ things you like to do in the fall.
* Read *N.C. Wyeth's Pilgrims* by Robert San Souci (Chronicle Books, 1991). Have students research an aspect of the first Thanksgiving.

Suggested Activities for Winter:

* Read *The Snowy Day* by Ezra Jack Keats (Viking, 1962).
  Writing prompt: What do you like to do on snowy days?
* Read *Penguin Pete* by Marcus Pfister (North-South Books, 1987).
  Writing prompt: Change the story. Tell about the day Steve taught Pete to fly.
* Read *The Black Snowman* by Phil Mendez (Scholastic, 1989).
  Writing prompt: Pretend you found a magic cloth. Tell about your adventure.

Suggested Activities for Spring/Summer:

- Share *In the Tall, Tall, Grass* by Denise Fleming (Henry Holt and Company, 1991). Writing prompt: *Write a silly story. Tell about animals who couldn't be hidden by the grass, like a kangaroo, or a giraffe. Tell what each would do. (Example: Kangaroo, hip hop)*
- Share *The Runaway Bunny* by Margaret Wise Brown (HarperCollins, 1942). Writing prompt: *If you ran away, where would you go and what would you do?*
- Share *Chicken Sunday* by Patricia Polacco (Philomel Books, 1992). Writing prompt: *Tell about a time you had to earn something you really wanted.*

Wrapping Paper Pocket

Create a pocket that corresponds to a particular subject or theme.

1. Cut a piece of 9" x 12" (23 cm x 30.5 cm) birthday wrapping paper.
2. Fold the paper to make a 6" x 9" (15.3 cm x 23 cm) pocket.
3. Attach the two sides.

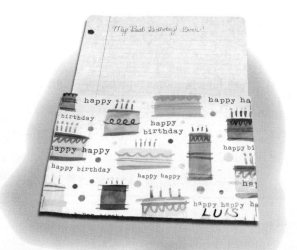

Suggested Activities:

- Have students write about the best birthdays they can remember.
- Have students plan the perfect birthday party.
- Have students describe how they hope their lives will be when they reach their 21st birthdays.

Variation:

Let students make individual decorated pockets out of the materials they choose. Attach pockets to a bulletin board titled "A Pocket Full of Dreams" or "A Pocket Full of Wishes." Read one of the following books to students, then have them write about dreams or wishes they have for the future of our planet and its inhabitants.

- *Three Wishes* by Harriet Ziefert (Puffin, 1996)
- *Whoever You Are* by Mem Fox (Voyager Books, 1997)
- *Rachel, The Story of Rachel Carson* by Amy Ehrlich (Harcourt Books, 2003)

Sometimes, students need to share more than the written word. The following projects contain space for students to include objects and/or additional information they want to share along with their writing. Choose the projects that best suit the needs of your students.

File Folder Pocket

1. Choose a plain or colorful file folder.
2. Write a student's name on the tab.
3. Attach a completed writing sheet to the tabbed side with paper clips.
4. Using double-sided tape, attach a resealable plastic bag to the bottom portion of the open file.
5. Let the student insert items related to the writing into the plastic bag, to be viewed by students as they read the writing piece.

The folder may be reused, simply by securing a new writing piece to the folder with paper clips and changing the items in the plastic bag. The open folder may be stapled or thumbtacked to a bulletin board or folded in order to be moved from place to place.

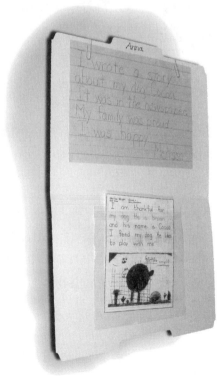

Suggested Activities:

- Discuss the five senses. Have students take a nature walk, paying attention to the things they see, touch, hear, and smell. Allow students to bring back an item, like a pinecone, leaf, flower, etc. Let students write about the experience and display the accompanying items in the plastic bags. (Note: Remind students to avoid potentially harmful plants during a nature walk. Also, students with plant and animal allergies should be especially cautious.)
- Have students write about their families. Ask students to bring pictures from home or draw pictures of their families to place in the bags.
- Assign pairs of students to interview each other. As a class, brainstorm a list of interview questions. Have each student write about the person he interviewed. The interviewer can take a photograph or draw a picture of his subject and place it inside the plastic bag.

Bags

All types of bags are great for containing writing projects. Projects included here can be created with plain paper bags, clear cellophane bags, decorated cellophane bags, and small bags with handles. Pick a bag, any bag!

Clear Cellophane Bag

1. Cut writing paper to fit inside the bag.
2. Have a student write the final draft on prepared paper.
3. Let her place related objects inside the bag.
4. Display bags as desired.

Variation:

Purchase cellophane bags with preprinted scenes that relate to the writing topics.

Suggested Activities:

- Let students write about things that are a specific color. Have students bring items from home that correspond to the specified color.

  Example: *A frog is green. Grass is green. Some apples are green. I have a green plastic rocket.* (The rocket would be placed in the bag.)

- Let students write their first names vertically along the left sides of the paper. Have students write a word or words on each line that describe themselves and that begins with the letter at the beginning of the line.

  Example:

    Sweet

    Helpful

    Eager to learn

    Likes to play softball

    Broke an arm last year

    Yells at her little sister!

  (Include a small drawing or photo of softball team, include a piece from her cast, etc.)

Small Paper Bag

1. Offer a variety of 5" x 11" (13 cm x 28 cm) colorful bags.
2. Standard writing paper may be used, or paper may be cut to fit the width of the bag.
3. Have students use paper clips or staples to attach completed writing to the open bags.
4. Let students place objects related to the writing subject inside the bags.

Suggested Activities:

*   Have each student write a description of an item placed inside the bag. Give other students the chance to read the description and guess the identity of the object.

*   Have students write descriptions in the form of riddles.

*   Let each student write a series of events or descriptive sentences to help students guess the identity of a topic.
    Example: The bunny leaves eggs. The flowers bloom. We wear new clothes. (Easter)

*   Students can place drawings, magazine pictures, or real objects inside the bag to represent the topics.

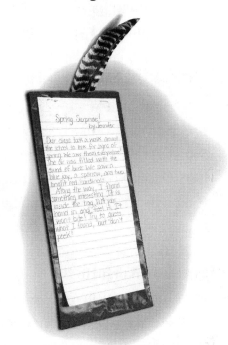

Handle Bag

Brown butcher paper bags with handles, 8" x 9" (20.3 cm x 23 cm), are sturdier than some other types of bags. Use these bags to hold larger, heavier items as well as smaller items.

1. Have students write about things that are special to them.
2. Attach the completed writing paper to the outside of the bags.
3. Let students place one or more items related to the writing topics inside the bags.

Suggested Activities:

- Put several bags in your writing center. In each bag, place an interesting picture taken from a catalog. Have each student choose a bag, take out the picture, and write what she thinks is happening in the picture. Change the pictures frequently.

- Invite a travel agent to visit and bring a selection of travel brochures. Or, collect a variety of brochures to bring to class. Have students browse through the brochures and choose places they would like to visit. Have each student write about the place he chose, storing the brochure in the bag.

- Have students write about the best places they have visited. Have each student place brochures, photos, or drawings of the place in the bag.

- Put several bags in your reading center. Place a book from your classroom library in each bag. Choose a variety of topics and reading levels. Place book review sheets in a tray in the center. Have each student choose a book to read, and complete a book review sheet to attach to the bag containing the book she read. (See **Book Review** sheet on page 57.) **Variation:** Have students write new endings to the books they have chosen to read. Attach the new endings to the bags. (See **New Ending** sheet on page 58.)

- Put three bags in your writing center. In one bag, place slips of paper that contain story characters. In another, place slips of paper containing story settings. In the third, place slips of paper containing story problems. Have students reach into each bag, without looking, to choose a slip of paper. Students will write stories using the characters, settings, and problems they have chosen. (See reproducibles on pages 59-64.)

Name _____ Date _____

Book Review

Title: _____

Author: _____

This book is about _____

_____

_____

My favorite character is _____

because _____

_____

My favorite part was _____

_____

_____

I would/would not (circle one) tell other people to read this book because

_____

_____

_____

Name _____   Date _____

New Ending

Title: _____

Author: _____

Main Character(s): _____

_____

Problem or conflict: _____

_____

My new ending: _____

_____

_____

_____

_____

_____

_____

_____

Characters

a pirate	a scarecrow
a family on vacation	a grandmother
two basketball players	a pizza delivery person
a fat cat	a talking pig
an astronaut	a six-foot-tall bunny
a detective	a 500-pound rat
a little girl	two teenage boys
a babysitter	the principal
the teacher	a snowman
a robot	a frog

Characters

a superhero	twins
a talking dog	an alien
an invisible person	a talking parade balloon
a pack of seals	soccer players
a singer	a scientist
three bugs	a king or queen
a mouse	a penguin
a cowboy	a 10-pound frog
the custodian	a substitute teacher
a yard gnome	a statue

 Classroom Publishing Toolbox • CD-104098 • © Carson-Dellosa

Settings

the zoo	a playground
Mars	the jungle
a ship	the park
the desert	the South Pole
a deserted island	the hospital
the shopping mall	the grocery store
a birthday party	an airplane
a train	a school
Australia	the school cafeteria
an ice skating rink	the moon

Settings

a submarine	a museum
the North Pole	talent show
an elevator	a racetrack
a carnival	in a phone booth
a tree house	a camper
swimming pool	inside a bottle
an igloo	a parade
a sports arena	the bottom of the ocean
inside a dollhouse	a roller rink
a candy store	a pumpkin patch

Classroom Publishing Toolbox • CD-104098 • © Carson-Dellosa

Conflicts (Problems) and Situations

enter a dance contest	wash a car
go canoeing	teach an exercise class
babysit triplets	fill in for sick cheerleaders
become furniture	compete on a game show
throw a party	learn to walk on a tightrope
eat very spicy food	play hockey
prepare a feast	enter a pie eating contest
learn how to fly	shrink
discover an old book	make a cake
teach a unicycle class	invent a machine

Conflicts (Problems) and Situations

move to a new place	can't find a way home
make a new friend	sing
lose all money	feel sick
can't talk	accidently eat a worm
go over a waterfall	falls down a large hole
find talking trees	need to buy a present
is mad at a friend	needs to get eyeglasses
work at a beauty shop	ride in a hot air balloon
meet a fairy tale character	go to camp
make the world's biggest pizza	find a lucky penny

Photo Sleeve

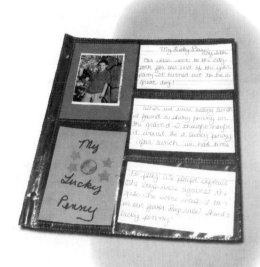

There are a variety of photo sleeves available at most stores that sell photo albums and/or scrapbooks. Some sleeves are divided into sections, while others contain one large area. Display individual sheets or combine into class books. Place the class books in your reading center for students to read again and again.

Suggested Activities:

- Share *I Like Me* by Nancy Carlson (Puffin Books, 1988). Have students write what they like about themselves. Include their photos or self-portraits.

- Have each student write about a special day or field trip. Use a sleeve divided into sections. (See above.) Have each student write the beginning of his story on one index card, the middle on a second index card, and the end on the third index card. Have him place the cards in order in the sections on the right side of the sleeve. Let him place a photo or drawing related to the story in one section on the left side of the sleeve. Then, let him place a memento of the trip in the other section on the left.

- Share *When I Was Young in the Mountains* by Cynthia Rylant (E.P. Dutton, 1982). Have students write about special things they remember about being younger. Let them place the writing along with mementos in the sleeves.

Manila Envelope

Suggested Activities:

- Place an envelope at your writing center. Attach several **Days of the Week** sheets to the front of the envelope with a binder clip. (See reproducible on page 67.) Write one day of the week on each of seven index cards. Place the index cards inside the envelope. Have students who come to the center remove and complete one **Days of the Week** sheet. Have them remove the index cards and place the days of the week in order.

- Make a present for a special person! Have students write letters on decorative stationery, thanking special people in their lives for all of the things they do to make life better. Attach the letters to the front of the envelopes. Give each student 10 index cards. Have the class brainstorm tasks they could do to show their special people how much they care. (Take out the trash, wash the dog, clean their rooms, etc.) On each card, have students list one thing they will do to show their appreciation to their special people. Have students place the cards inside the envelopes. The students should take their envelopes home. A special person can choose a card, when desired, and the student will do the task listed on the card.

- Have students write reports about people connected with a current unit of study. Attach the reports to the front of the envelopes. Have each student write an important event found in the report on each of five index cards. Let students place the index cards in the envelopes. Have students exchange envelopes with partners. Each student should read the partner's report, take out the cards, and put the events in order, referring to the report to check for accuracy.

Classroom Publishing Toolbox • CD-104098 • © Carson-Dellosa

Days of the Week

On Monday, I like to _____.

On Tuesday, I like to _____.

On Wednesday, I like to _____.

On Thursday, I like to _____.

On Friday, I like to _____.

On Saturday, I like to _____.

On Sunday, I like to _____.

Bakery Box

Small, inexpensive bakery boxes are available at most paper goods stores. Or, ask a local bakery to donate boxes for your class.

Suggested Activities:

- Have students write autobiographies. Attach the completed writing to the inside of the tops of the boxes. Have students create collages of photos to attach to the inside bottoms of the boxes, or let students bring items representing their lives to place inside the boxes. Let students decorate the outside of the boxes as desired.
- Share *Dinosaur Days* by Joyce Milton (Random House, 1985) or *Dinosaurs* by Gail Gibbons (Scholastic, 1987). Have students research specific dinosaurs and write reports. Have students make clay dinosaurs. Let students place the clay dinosaurs in the boxes and attach the reports as described above.
- Have students choose topics to research that are related to a current unit of study. Have students write their reports to attach as described above. Have students create word searches or crossword puzzles based on information stated in the reports. Make copies to place in the boxes. Place the boxes in a center. As students go to the center, have them choose boxes of interest, read the reports, and complete the puzzles.

Book/Tape Packet

Let students create small books and record their writing on audiotapes. Combine the books and tapes in resealable plastic bags. Label the outside of the bags to identify each student's work.

Suggested Activities:

- Display the bags in your classroom reading center for students to enjoy throughout the year.
- Create a check-out system to allow students to take packages home overnight and share the writing of fellow students. That's reading practice, as well!
- Find a fellow teacher who will allow students to create the same type of packages. Exchange sets and give your students the opportunity to share their writing with others, and read what schoolmates are writing.

Other Types of Publishing

25 FT.

PREMIUM GRADE
HEAVY DUTY TAPE MEASURE

1" WIDE x 25' LONG

There are so many ways to publish! Remember, publishing simply means sharing completed work with others. Young children may share lists of rhyming words or words that begin with the same initial consonant. Students may write an original play or song and share it with another class or with the entire student body. Students can write poems to be published in the section of the local newspaper that focuses on schools. Publishing does not have to be involved or cumbersome. You already guide students to write a variety of pieces on a daily basis. As you plan lessons, think of ways to incorporate some type of writing activity. Not every writing piece will be published. Let students choose special pieces once in a while. Have students "spiff" those pieces up a little and share them with anybody and everybody.

Invitation

Invite visitors to your classroom throughout the year. Make invitations for students to deliver to guests.

Making an Invitation

1. Choose one of the patterns found on pages 71-73 for a 4" x 7" (10.2 cm x 17.8 cm) invitation. Copy it onto colorful paper.
2. Fill in the information to include the reason for the invitation, date, time, and place.
3. Decorate the invitation as desired.

Reproducibles

Sample Invitations
(page 71-73)

Newspaper Patterns
(page 91-99)

Interview Questions
(page 100)

Writing a Haiku
(page 103)

Talk Show Interview Questions
(page 107)

Making an Envelope

1. Fold an 8½" x 11" (21.5 cm x 28 cm) sheet of white paper in about ½" (1.3 cm) on both sides.

2. Fold the bottom of the paper up toward the top about 4" (10.2 cm).

3. Unfold and place pieces of double-stick tape along the two open sides. Refold and secure the sides.

4. Place another small piece of double-stick tape or a small square used to hold photos in the center of the flap.

5. Insert the invitation.

6. Close the flap by folding it over the envelope.

7. Decorate the envelope and let students deliver the invitation.

Suggested Activities:

- Have a "Grandparents" or "My Special Person" Day. Have each student invite someone to spend a morning with him at school, learning what that student does at school each day. End with light refreshments and a sharing time of student writing.

- Invite school helpers (cafeteria workers, custodian, secretary) in for punch and cookies. Let students share writing about how and why school helpers are important. (Before completing any food activity, ask families' permission and inquire about students' food allergies and religious or other preferences.)

- Have a class discussion about an issue of importance facing the school. Maybe a decision is being made about wearing school uniforms or allowing vending machines on campus. Have students write their opinions regarding the outcome of the issue. Invite members of the school board to come and hear what students have to say and to discuss the issue further.

Sample Invitations

Please join us for _____

Place: _____

Date: _____

Time: _____

We hope to see you there!

Please join us for _____

Place: _____

Date: _____

Time: _____

We hope to see you there!

Sample Invitations

Please join us for _____

Place: _____

Date: _____

Time: _____

We hope to see you there!

Please join us for _____

Place: _____

Date: _____

Time: _____

We hope to see you there!

Sample Invitations

Please join us for _____

Place: _____

Date: _____

Time: _____

We hope to see you there!

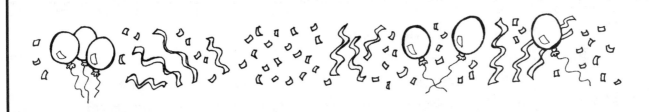

Please join us for _____

Place: _____

Date: _____

Time: _____

We hope to see you there!

Tri-Fold Travel Brochure

1. Choose a piece of sturdy construction paper. It should be at least 9" x 13" (23 cm x 33 cm).
2. Fold each side in to meet in the center.
3. Have a student write information about her trip on the inside center panel.
4. Let her draw corresponding illustrations on each side.
5. Let her attach brochures from a travel agency or Chamber of Commerce, if available, to outside panels with paper clips.

Suggested Activities:

• Have young students tell about places in town they like to visit and why. Perhaps a student likes to go to a certain bakery on Saturday mornings. A student might like to visit a particular toy store in town, or perhaps there is a park a student's family visits often.

• Have students pretend a new person is moving to town. Let them choose places of interest the new person should know about. Have them explain why these places are fun or interesting, or unique to your town.

• Let each student choose a destination related to a current unit of study or a place he would like to visit. Have students write to request information. Also, free travel information for numerous destinations can be found on the Internet. Let students use the information to create tri-fold brochures. Have students share their information orally with classmates.

Poster

Suggested Activities:

• Have students create posters rather than tri-fold brochures to tell about special places to visit.
• Let students create imaginary places they think would be fun to visit.
• Have students write reports regarding a current unit of study and include drawings, pictures, or collages related to the topics.

Spiral Writing

1. Make copies of the spiral template below after enlarging 200%.
2. Beginning at the center of the spiral and turning the pages as they write, have students write their stories on the lines.
3. Let students cut on the lines if desired.

Suggested Activities:

• Have students write about their favorite candy. Let students glue a dowel or craft stick to the back of the spiral to make the writing look like lollipops.
• Have students write the lyrics to songs that are sung in rounds.
• Students can make their own wind catchers by cutting the spiral on the lines. Let students punch holes in the center sections and attach string for hanging.
• Have students make lists, separated by commas, of things that go in a circle or spin.

Hanger Writing (Beginning, Middle, and End)

1. Have each student review a writing piece and identify the beginning, middle, and end of the piece.
2. Have her write each sections on a separate sheet of lined paper.
3. Help her attach the beginning to a green sheet of construction paper, the middle to a yellow sheet of construction paper, and the ending to a red piece of construction paper.
4. Let her connect the three sheets from top to bottom, in order: green at the top, yellow in the middle, and red at the bottom.
5. Have her tape the green sheet to a coat hanger.

Suggested Activities:

- Compare writing to a stoplight. Explain that green means go. It is the beginning of the story. Yellow means caution. Be careful to say all of the important things you want to share. The story is in the middle. Red is stop. The story needs an end.
- Have students write the steps for washing clothes. Allow students to "hang up" their writing when they are finished.
- Have each student write about three or more things he does when he "hangs out" with his friends. Students should write each event on the separate pieces of paper. Encourage students to use transition words when moving from one event to another.

Framing

1. Choose a shape related to a theme or unit of study.
2. Determine the size needed to accommodate writing paper.
3. Create a template from a sturdy material, such as poster board or cardboard.
4. Trace the shape onto construction paper or other chosen material and cut out.
5. Cut out a center square or rectangle large enough to display a page of student writing.
6. Place the shape over completed writing.
7. Glue the shape into place.
8. Decorate the shape to reflect the theme of writing.

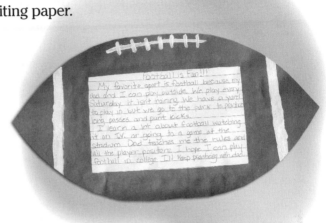

Suggested Activities:

- Share *A House Is a House for Me* by Mary Ann Hoberman (Puffin, 1982). Talk about the variety of houses presented in the book, both serious and silly, such as nest for a bird and the husks for an ear of corn. Have students write about the houses they live in or about the houses they hope to have someday. Frame the writing with house shapes.

- Study animals and their habitats. Provide patterns for a variety of animal homes. Have students choose animals and write about their homes and habitats. Have young students draw pictures and write words to tell about the animals. Frame the writing with animals' homes.

- Study community helpers. Provide frames of important buildings in a community, such as the library, school, hospital, firehouse, police station, etc. Have students write about the services provided by people who choose those careers.

- During a unit study on nutrition, create frames of fruits and vegetables. Have each student choose one, use the five senses to describe it, and tell why it is part of a healthy diet.

- Have each student choose a favorite sport that involves a ball. Create a frame to represent each (basketball, football, soccer ball, softball, dodgeball, tennis ball, beach ball, etc.). Have each student explain how to play the game and/or why she likes to play. Title the writing display "We're Having a Ball!"

Tops and Bottoms

1. Choose a shape related to a theme or unit of study. (The shape should be wide enough to cover the widths of the top and bottom of writing paper.)
2. Create a template from sturdy material, such as poster board or cardboard.
3. Trace the shape onto chosen material and cut out.
4. Let students decorate cut-out top and bottom.
5. Staple or glue the pieces to the top and bottom of a page of completed student writing so that the writing page becomes the center of the shape.

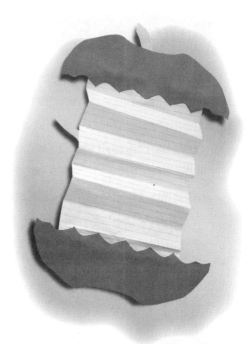

Suggested Activities:

• Share an age-appropriate book, song, or story about apples, such as *Apples* by Gail Gibbons (Holiday House, 2001) or *Apple Picking Time* by Michelle Benoit Slawson (Random House Children's Books, 1998). Have students write about the growth of an apple from seed to fruit.

• Slice and share at least three varieties of apples. Let students draw and write about the varieties they like best. (Before completing any food activity, ask families' permission and inquire about students' food allergies and religious or other preferences.)

• Have young students cut, paste, and label pictures of objects that begin with the short /a/ sound.

• Create a template for the top and bottom of an acorn. Have students cut, paste, and label objects with the long /a/ sound.

• Practice Beginning, Middle, and End. Create a template shape for a wide pencil top and bottom. Have each student write the beginning of a story or report at the top of the pencil, the middle on a sheet of writing paper, and the end on the bottom. Let students make up their own stories or follow a story prompt written on the top pencil piece. Display on a bulletin board titled "We Get to the Point."

• Create a rocket ship template during a unit study of neighborhoods and communities. Have students write about what it might be like to live on the moon someday. Who else would live on the moon? Creatures from another planet? What would they look like? Where would you live? What would you eat? How would you travel from place to place? What kind of jobs would there be?

Mixing Bowl and Spoon

1. Create a template of a mixing bowl large enough for students to write on or large enough to accommodate a piece of writing paper. Also, create a template of a wooden spoon.

2. Let students trace and cut out bowls and spoons from colorful construction paper or from other materials of your choice. If students will write directly on the mixing bowls, be sure they choose a light color of construction paper for the mixing bowl.

When I have a bad day, I can read a funny book to get me back in a good mood.

3. If students will write on sheets of paper, have them glue or staple the completed paper onto the mixing bowls.

4. After writing, let students decorate the bowls and spoons.

Suggested Activities:

- Prepare a spoon with the following prompt for each student: *When I feel mad I will . . .* Share *Mean Soup* by Betsy Everitt (Harcourt, Brace & Company, 1995). Discuss positive ways to let off steam after a bad day or when frustrated by the actions of another. Give each student a mixing bowl and spoon. Have students draw pictures and/or write on the mixing bowls the strategies they will use to deal with angry feelings in a positive way. Place the spoons alongside the bowls. Display the bowls and spoons on a bulletin board titled "Mixing Up a Good Mood."

- Have students write on the spoons a "tired" word, such as *said* or *went*. Have a class discussion or let students use an age-appropriate thesaurus to make a class list of more descriptive words. ***Example:*** *went: trotted, skipped, strolled, ran*, etc. Have the students write the list on the bowls. Display the words for student reference when writing. Title the display "Cooking Up Descriptive Words."

Double Front Flap

1. Enlarge the boy and girl patterns on page 81 to desired size. Then, make copies for students. Give each student a boy or girl pattern.

2. Have students write on the torso area of the patterns and cut out the pieces.

3. Have students place the patterns over construction paper and trace. Let students cut out these pieces.

4. Instruct students to cut the construction paper torso sections in half vertically.

5. Let them place construction paper halves over the torsos with students' writing on them, matching the edges.

6. Let students punch one hole in the top left and right corners of the torso sections.

7. Have students attach with paper fasteners, then open flaps to reveal students' writing.

8. Let students glue arms, legs, and head to the back of the torso section.

Suggested Activities:

- Have students write words and phrases that tell about themselves: *happy, fun, sweet, brown hair*, etc.

- Have students complete an "All About Me" form that might include the following:

  My name is _____.   I like to play_____.

  I am _____ years old.   Sometimes I am happy when _____.

  My hair is _____ and my eyes are _____.   I wish _____.

  I like to eat _____.   My favorite book is _____.

- Let each student secretly choose a classmate about whom she will write three positive statements. Give students an opportunity to share the writing before it is attached to the figure and have classmates attempt to guess the identity of the classmate.

- Have students write about people who are important in their lives.

- Let students write about school staff and faculty. Place the figures in the hallway for all to enjoy!

Boy and Girl Patterns

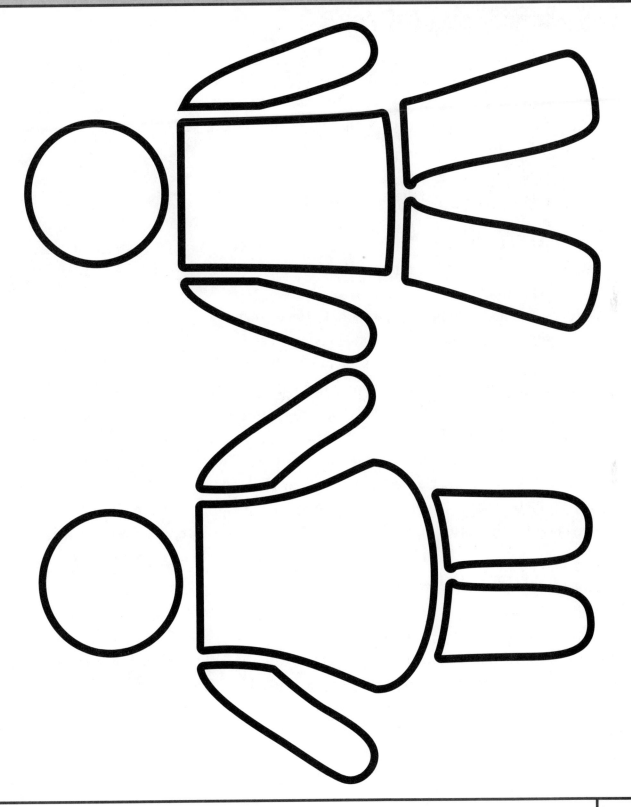

Magnifying Glass

1. Create a template for a large magnifying glass with handle.
2. Have students write directly on the magnifying glasses. Or, cut out circles of white construction paper sized to cover most of the circular part of the magnifying glass. Have students write on the circles.
3. Attach completed writing to the magnifying glasses.

Suggested Activities:

- Have students write the steps taken in a class science experiment.

- Let students read a simple mystery book. Have them write the title on the handles of the magnifying glasses. Then, have students determine Who?, When?, Where?, and What happened? in the story. Students should write their answers in the center of the magnifying glasses. Display the magnifying glasses. Display the magnifying glasses. Title the display "We're Checking It Out!"

- Create a crossword puzzle related to a unit of study. Trim completed puzzles to fit on the surface of the magnifying glasses. Title a display "Figuring Out the Clues."

- Create a bulletin board or center area entitled "Super Sleuths Solve the Mystery." Place four to five magnifying glasses on the board. Attach a different story starter to each. Let each student choose one and complete the story on a separate sheet of paper. Place completed stories around the magnifying glasses.

Can Glyphs

1. Collect one clean, empty can for each student in class.
2. Cut construction paper into strips that will fit around the cans.
3. Have students complete glyphs on the construction paper strips and decorate as desired
4. Let students cover the cans with the pieces of construction paper by gluing them in place.
5. Write the name of the student on a piece of paper and place inside the can for identification.

Glyphs are pictorial representations of information. Assemble a three-dimensional graph by having students display representations of their eye colors, siblings, and their modes of transportation to school. Display the following on the board or on a chart.

Eye Color		Siblings		Transportation to School	
Blue	○○○○	None	♥ ♥ ♥ ♥	Walk	✚ ✚ ✚ ✚
Brown	☐☐☐☐	One	| | | |	Car	▼ ▼ ▼ ▼
Green	△ △ △ △	Two	∧∧∧∧	Bus	✳ ✳ ✳ ✳
Other	◇ ◇ ◇ ◇	More	M M M M	Other	◆ ◆ ◆ ◆

Suggested Activities:

- Have students who share the same characteristics stack their cans together. Which stack is the tallest? Shortest?
- Have students write about the things they have in common with their clasmates.
- Have students write one thing that makes them unique from all of their other classmates.
- In your computer center, read the story *The First Totem Pole* by Roas Bell (http://www.virtualmuseum. ca/Exhibitions/Haida/java/english/totem/index.html) to students. Have students write short summaries about the story and place it inside their can glyphs.

Story Chain

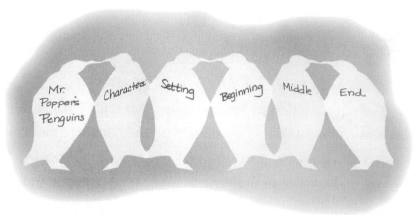

1. Choose a simple shape of an object related to a theme or unit of study.
2. Make the object large enough to allow for student writing on each piece in the series.
3. Cut a piece of light colored butcher paper 6" x 24" (15 cm x 61 cm) long for each student.
4. Let the student make a 4" (10.2 cm) fold at one end of the paper strip, then accordion fold the paper to the opposite edge of the strip.
5. Have the student trace the template onto the top section.
6. Help her cut out the shape, being careful not to cut the folded edges of the paper.
7. Let her unfold the chain and decorate with markers, paints, wiggly eyes, sequins, bits of lace, wool and ribbon, or anything else you have on hand.

Suggested Activities:

- Outline of a person: Have students draw a picture or write on each shape to sequence important events in the life of a famous person.
- Tennis shoe: Have students write directions for completing processes (how to play a game, steps in a recipe, how to do the backstroke, how to ride a bike, etc.) that are of interest to them. Title a display "We've Got the Steps Down."

  Variation for character education: Have students write rules for good behavior, ways to handle conflict, positive methods for handling personal anger, etc. Title the display "We're Taking the Right Steps."
- Choose a simple shape related to the theme or unit of study:
  - Write a word on the first shape and write a rhyming word on each additional shape.
  - Write a word on the first shape and write a synonym on each additional shape.
  - Write an animal on the first shape and write a fact about the animal on each additional shape.

Fabric Squares

Many craft, hobby, or fabric stores carry inexpensive material that can be cut into squares and used as scarves or bandanas. Some stores even have readymade bandanas in a variety of colors and themed prints. If you choose to buy fabric to cut, remember you can cut the fabric with pinking shears to give it a finished edge. Students may choose to decorate plain fabric with fabric paint.

I would fly to the circus and ride the elephant
Anna

Suggested Activities:

- Have students imagine places they would like to visit if they had magic bandanas that would whisk them instantly to any place in the world when they were around their necks. Let students wear bandanas while they draw or write about the places they would like to visit. Let students illustrate their faces on paper plates. Staple the writing pages to the bottoms of the paper plates. Tie the bandanas around the bottoms of the plates and staple to the plate. (See photo.)

- Have students imagine the magic bandana would change them into anyone they wish to be. Who would they choose to be and why? Maybe they would choose to remain themselves. In that case, what additional abilities would they wish to have?

- Help students begin to distinguish between "wants" and "needs." Give each student a bandana. Ask him to imagine he is going on a journey and may never come back. He is only allowed to take as many items as the bandana will hold, so he should only take items he really needs. Have students list things they want to take, then have a class discussion about each item, categorizing each under the heading of Wants or Needs. Have students write about the things they eventually choose to take and why those items are so important. Take a walk around the school to allow each student to find a stick he can use to hold his bandana. Tie the opposite ends of the bandana together to form a bundle and tie the bandana to the stick. Roll the writing page, tie it with yarn, and place it inside the bandana. Place bundles in a center and let students read each other's writing.

Fun with Foam

Many hobby and craft shops carry inexpensive sheets of colorful foam that can be easily cut with a pair of scissors. These foam sheets come in a variety of sizes and colors. Pre-cut foam pieces in a variety of shapes are also available. Some even come backed with self-stick material. All you need to do is peel off the paper backing and stick the shape where desired. No scissors . . . no glue . . . no mess!

Suggested Activities:

- Share *Grandfather Tang's Story* by Ann Tompert (Bantam Doubleday Dell Books for Young Readers, 1997). Have students cut freehand shapes, trace shape patterns, and cut, or use pre-cut shapes like those in the story or any shapes they wish. Have students glue the shapes onto light-colored construction paper, leaving space at the bottom of the page for writing about their creations. Students may wish to add illustrations to complete their pictures.

- Have each student use a fine tipped permanent marker to write a short story or report on a separate sheet of paper. After editing, have the student transfer the story onto a light-colored piece of foam. Then, let the student cut the foam story into six to eight pieces, creating a story puzzle. Store puzzles in resealable, plastic bags. Place the stories in the reading center and allow students to put together and read classmates' stories.

- Make bookmarks. Cut foam strips wide enough to accommodate a small amount of student writing. Have students write the following, "My favorite book is _____ because _____ ." Let students decorate their bookmarks as desired.

- Decorate writing by creating foam borders. Glue foam cutouts around the border or use pinking shears or craft scissors to cut long foam strips to glue around the border.

- Combine math and writing. Have students create a pattern with foam shapes and write the directions. ***Example:*** "My pattern is one green heart, one red square, and two yellow circles." Then, let each student glue the foam pattern to the bottom of the paper.

Eggs

Use colorful plastic eggs as a publishing tool. Allow students to draw or write, then fold the writing and encase them in the eggs.

Suggested Activities:

- Have students write or illustrate words that include the short /e/ sound. (*leg, red, bed, men, ten, step, net, pet, elephant, egg*, etc.)
- Share *An Extraordinary Egg* by Leo Lionni (Bantam Doubleday Dell Books for Young Readers, 1998). Use a fine-tipped permanent marker to write an egg-related story prompt on the outside of each egg or write the prompt on a piece of paper and place it inside the egg. Use the same prompt several times if desired. Place the eggs in a basket. Title the display "A Basket of Egg Stories." (See photo.) Let each student choose an egg, and write to the story prompt. When students finish, have them fold the stories and place them in the eggs.
- Collect the eggs in the basket. Choose a few stories to share with the class each day or place the basket in a center and allow students to read each other's writing.

Examples of Story Prompts:

- While digging in the woods, I found a dinosaur egg.
- I found a purple, polka-dotted egg under the back porch.
- A golden egg fell out of the nest in the tall tree in our front yard.
- Mike threw a red and orange striped egg at me.
- A bird dropped her egg into my lap.
- The black egg at the museum started to crack!

- Share *The Emperor's Egg* by Martin Jenkins (Candlewick Press, 1998) to teach students about the life cycle of a chick. Have students write about the process and place the writing inside eggs.

Paper Airplane

1. Have students fold an 8½" x 11" (21.5 cm x 28 cm) paper in half lengthwise.
2. Instruct them to fold the top corner back toward the center fold, creating a right triangle. Have them repeat on the opposite side.
3. Have them fold outside edges of paper back toward the folded seam and crease to create wings.
4. Have students unfold the planes and write in the center section.
5. Have students write the titles of their writing on the wings.
6. Paper clip airplanes onto a, line strung across the room.

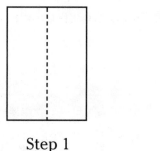   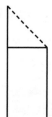   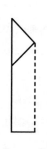

Step 1   Step 2   Step 3

Suggested Activities:

- Have students write and illustrate compound words. Let them write the first word on one wing and the second word on the other wing. Have them write and illustrate the compound word on the inside of the plane. ***Example:*** *airplane, backpack, cupcake, campfire,* etc.
- Visit the airport. Let students write about the experience.
- Let students write about faraway places they would like to visit.
- During a unit on careers, invite a pilot to visit and tell about her job. Have students write reports.
- Have students write the steps in making a paper airplane.

Classroom Newspaper

Print all the news that's fit to print! Create a classroom newspaper that is compiled once each month. To get students in the spirit, share *The Furry News: How to Make a Newspaper* by Loreen Leedy (Holiday House, 1996) or *Deadline! From News to Newspaper* by Gail Gibbons (HarperCollins Childrens Books, 1987). Spend some time with students reviewing the local newspaper to discuss sections you may wish to include in your class newspaper. As a class, decide what your paper will include. Your newspaper can be fairly simple and easy to create. Each month, divide students into groups and have each group write for a specific section. Will there be an editorial section? A fashion section? A cartoon section? Will students include illustrations or photographs along with articles? Consider including the following:

- **Class News:** Write about field trips, units of study, visitors, special events, new students, etc.
- **School News:** Write about sporting events, cultural events, changes in teaching staff, etc. Each month, interview a faculty member. (See the **Interview Questions** reproducible on page 100.) Consider any issue that affects the school as a whole.
- **Editorial:** Debate the pros and cons of an issue confronting your school. It may be as simple as being allowed to wear shorts to school on hot days or as complex as steps that need to be taken in order to ensure student safety.
- **Weather:** Pair students to contribute to this section. Have one student take daily notes on weather conditions and tally the number of rainy days, sunny days, etc. Have the other student use the information to write an article that summarizes the weather for the month.
- **Book Reviews**: Have students write about books read during the month. The class may wish to invent a scale for rating each book: 5 stars = great reading; 1 star = the pits!
- **Movie/Video Reviews**: Have students write about movies or videos they have seen and can recommend to other families.

Your class may decide to include other sections. Blank templates are provided on pages 98-99.

Your newspaper does not have to be written in columns. You may simply create a title page, make a heading sheet to identify the beginning of each section, and place all completed writing sheets pertaining to that section behind the heading sheet. Add the next heading sheet and continue in the same manner until all sections have been compiled, similar to compiling the pages for a book. Bind the sheets as desired. You may wish to punch holes and place the pages in a three-ring binder.

Variation:

Copy one of the Newspaper templates on pages 91-97 or create your own using pages 98-99. Have students write the titles of their articles in the text box at the top. Students should write the final copies of their articles on the reproducible sheets. Use additional sheets as necessary. Make copies of every student's article. Combine all student articles and place a cover sheet on the front for students to decorate if desired. Bind the newspaper and give each child a copy of the class newspaper.

Suggested Activities:

- Place the three-ring binder containing the newspaper articles in your reading center for students to enjoy.
- Let each student have an opportunity during the month to take the binder home overnight to share with family.
- Add a new binder each month, creating a newspaper section in your reading center.
- Send a copy of the newspaper to each class in the school. Ask students to let your class know of any events that should be included in the School News section of the next edition.
- Ask the media specialist to place a copy in the library for students to read when they visit the library.
- Send a copy to the local newspaper to be included in their section about what's happening in local schools.

There is information on the Internet to lead you through the steps of designing and publishing a classroom newspaper with the help of your computer. This Internet site includes information posted by educators who are willing to share their expertise: **http://208.183.128.3/tutorials/ indexnews.html.** The Web site is for users of Microsoft Word and gives directions about how to create an electronic newspaper to view on the Internet.

At this site, you can access the following menu items:

- Using a Word Processor
- Getting Started
- Putting It Together
- Newsworthy Sites
- Creating an Electronic Newspaper
- Finding Web Space

Class News

School News

Movie Review

Classroom Publishing Toolbox • CD-104098 • © Carson-Dellosa

Book Review

Weather

Classroom Publishing Toolbox • CD-104098 • © Carson-Dellosa

Upcoming Events

Interview Questions

1. Name of person being interviewed: _____

_____

2. What is your job at our school? _____

_____

3. How long have you been at our school? _____

4. What do you like best about your job? _____

_____

_____

5. What would you change about our school? _____

_____

_____

6. What else would you like to share about your job? _____

_____

_____

Thank you for telling me about yourself and about your job at our school!

Pop-Open Door

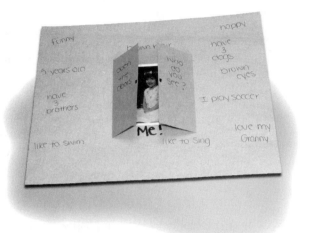

1. Select two pieces of 8½" x 11" (21.5 cm x 28 cm) construction paper.
2. Trace a 4" (10.2 cm) square in the center of the top sheet.
3. Draw a line from top to bottom through the center of the square.
4. Use a sharp instrument to cut along the top and bottom edges of the square.
5. Cut along the line drawn through the center from top to bottom.
6. Fold back the flaps.
7. Glue the top piece of construction paper to the back piece.
8. Fold the flaps back to reveal the inside.

Suggested Activities:

- Have each student draw a self-portrait to glue inside the flaps or let her glue a small photograph inside. Leave about 1" (2.5 cm) of space on both sides and at the bottom for writing. Have students write words or phrases to describe themselves and their personalities and their likes and dislikes. On the front of the left door flap, have students write "Open the doors." On the front of the right flap, have them write "Who do you see?" On the inside, have them write "Me!" under the photographs or self-portraits. Instruct students to write their first names down the left sides of the photos or self-portraits. Have students write their last names down the right sides of the photos or self-portraits.
- Have students place pictures or drawings of their families inside. Let them write words or phrases to describe their families.
- Have students describe famous people related to a current unit of study. Let them place drawings or pictures of the people inside the doors.
- Have students list the characteristics of animals from a current unit of study and include drawings or photos of the animals on the inside.

Haiku Fan

Haiku is a form of Japanese poetry. It often centers around subjects found in nature. The poem consists of three lines. The first line contains five syllables, the second line has seven syllables, and the third line has five syllables.

Example:

Summer

I see the blue sky.

The wind is softly blowing.

Summertime is here!

Share examples of haiku with students by reading *Don't Step on the Sky: A Handful of Haiku* by Miriam Chaikin (Henry Holt & Company, 2002) or *Red Dragonfly on My Shoulder: Haiku* by Sylvia Cassedy (Harper Collins, 1992).

Combine two artifacts of Japanese culture by writing a haiku on a Japanese fan. Have students use the Writing a Haiku template on page 103 to create their poems. Let them write the final version of the poems on the fan material. Then, instruct students to fold the fan as directed below. Attach the fans to a bulletin board with pushpins.

1. Choose a 9" x 13" (23 cm x 33 cm) piece of light colored construction paper or cut a piece of sturdy, colorful wrapping paper to the same size.
2. Fold the paper in half, as if making a book.
3. Have students open and write the completed haiku on the wrapping paper.
4. If using construction paper, let students decorate the blank side as desired.
5. Tell students how to accordion fold the paper to create a fan.
6. Have students gather and staple the bottom folds to create a handle.
7. If extra strength is needed to keep fan from flopping over, staple a strip of poster board to each side, along the handle.

Name _____ Date _____

 # Writing a Haiku

Think about something in nature you want to write about. Here are some ideas to consider:

- The wind
- Trees
- Weather (a sunny day, a rainy day, snow, fog)
- A particular animal
- Seasons

I will write about _____

The first line should have 5 syllables.

_____

The second line should have 7 syllables.

_____

The last line should have 5 syllables.

_____

Play

Give students an opportunity to write and perform a play. After all, there's no business like show business! Now, don't become overwhelmed at the thought of such a grand undertaking. The process can really be quite simple. Students write what they want to say based on the story line, they practice saying their parts, and they perform for themselves and/or others. If possible, invite families to view the performance. Families enjoy everything their children accomplish!

Suggested Activities:

- For younger students, create dialogue based on the information written on a predictable chart. A predictable chart is part of a structured language experience in which each student dictates a sentence relevant to the topic as you write the sentence on a large chart. At the end of the sentence, write the student's name in parentheses to acknowledge the author of the sentence. Each student focuses only on learning the words contained in his sentence. It is called a predictable chart because each sentence begins in the same way. A predictable chart can be based on almost any topic relevant to the class, from favorite foods to the value of rain, to the fun they had on the field trip to the farm.

Our Trip to the Farm
At the farm, I saw a goat. (Robert)
At the farm, I saw two pigs. (Sue)
At the farm, I drove a tractor. (Alan)
At the farm, I milked a cow. (Ling)
At the farm, I fed the chickens. (Ryan)
At the farm, I played in dirt. (Seth)
At the farm, I saw six cats. (Jeannine)
At the farm, I saw an old car. (Jon)
At the farm, I planted a tree. (Sarah)
At the farm, I collected eggs. (Nick)
At the farm, I saw lots of tools. (Gary)
At the farm, I dug in the dirt. (Rudy)
At the farm, I harvested corn. (Ashley)
At the farm, I carved a pumpkin. (Sierra)

- Take a current unit of study, such as the celebration of Earth Day. As closure to your study, create a predictable chart to help students sum up what they have learned. Take dictation for the chart during one class lesson. The next day, have each student practice reading his sentence from the chart. Continue each day, until you feel each student can read his sentence correctly.

For the play, have each student copy his own sentence onto a sentence strip. Decide how you will create a focus character for the play. For Earth Day, you might have a student dress as Mother Earth. She might be sad because she thinks no one cares about the earth because of pollution, etc. One student could ask, "Mother Earth, why are you crying?" Mother Earth might reply, "I am crying because no one cares about taking care of the earth. No one thinks the earth is important anymore." The class would answer, "We care about the earth. We'll tell you why." Then, each student would approach Mother Earth, carrying her sentence strip and read her sentence. At the end, Mother Earth would say, "I know you will help take care of the earth. Thank you for making me happy again." After the play, put sentence strips in a pocket chart in your reading center or hang the original predictable chart. Students will enjoy reading the sentences again and again.

Stage this simple play by choosing a topic, creating a predictable chart, having students learn their sentences, and providing an opportunity for a performance!

- For older students, let them help brainstorm scenarios for the play. Using the same example of Earth Day, students might suggest that aliens plan to destroy earth because they don't think anyone cares. Or, they might suggest Mother Earth plans to go underground and that there will never be seasons again, only continuous winter, because she doesn't think people are worth her trouble as they do not appreciate the beauty of the earth by keeping it clean. Set the parameters as with the younger students. Have one or two focus characters. All other students respond to the focus character(s). Have each student write only one or two sentences to contribute to the play. Kindly listen to all offerings, suggesting changes when needed. Older students may wish to create props and costumes to enhance the presentation of the play.

Talk Show Interview

Give older students an enjoyable opportunity to share what they have learned about famous people the class has studied. Brainstorm a list of people about whom students may choose to write. Have each student whisper the name of his chosen person to you. If the person has previously been chosen or is not appropriate, have the student make another choice. Give each student a copy of the Talk Show Interview Questions found on page 107. Have students conduct research, if necessary, to be able to answer the questions as if they are the chosen people. Choose a student to be the host of the show. Set a chair and table at the front of the room to resemble the staging of a talk show. Introduce the host, then introduce the participating student as the "Mystery Guest." Have the host ask the interview questions. At any point in the interview, students in the "audience" may guess the identity of the "Mystery Guest." They must explain why they think the information corresponds to the identity of the "Mystery Guest."

You may need to continue the Talk Show over several days. Each day, choose a different student to serve as Talk Show host.

Talk Show Interview Questions

1. Are you still living? _____

2. If not, when did you die? _____

3. Are you famous in sports? _____

4. Are you famous for your music? _____

5. Are you famous for your contributions to science? _____

6. Are you famous for your participation in government? _____

7. Tell us some important things about your life. _____

   _____

   _____

   _____

8. Why do you think you are still important today? _____

   _____

   _____

9. Who would like to guess the identity of our Mystery Guest?

Song

Bring some original music into the classroom. Throughout the year, let students create original words to go along with tunes your class already knows. The topic of the song may relate to a unit of study, or it may be just for fun.

Examples: Sung to the tune of "I'm a Little Teapot"

I'm a little green frog.
Watch me hop.
I can jump and never stop.
When I see a cool pond
Then I grin.
Just take a leap and dive right in!

I'm a smart third grader.
Watch me think.
I can multiply, quick as a wink.
When I need a math fact
I don't strain.
I pull it right out of my brain!

Suggested Activity:

- Give students a topic and a choice of tunes. Divide them into small groups. Let each group write a song and sing it for the class. Have students work as a class or in small groups throughout the year to create new songs. Make copies of the songs to include in a class songbook. Give each student a copy of the songbook at the end of the year. If possible, record students singing each song onto an audiocassette. Have duplicates made and give each child a copy to accompany the songbook.

Integrating Technology and Classroom Publishing

Ah, technology . . . a blessing to some and a bane to others. It seems that everywhere we turn, we are inundated with newer, better, and faster ways to accomplish tasks with the help of technology. It is true that we have the opportunity to expose students to a much broader world view thanks to the World Wide Web. However, there is a tremendous variance among school districts as to the types of technology available to classroom teachers as well as the depth of training provided to help them feel comfortable using the technology they do have at hand. Just think, some teachers have no access to computers. Some have one computer for the class to share. Other teachers are fortunate enough to have multiple computers in the classroom or access to a computer lab. And, some schools have computer labs connected to the Internet, that are managed by technology instructors who work with teachers to plan lessons related to classroom study.

No matter how limited your resources, there are ways to integrate some level of technology into the publishing process. If you have a computer in your classroom, you may already have a simple word processing program installed that will allow your students to type and print their writing. Your media specialist may have some publishing programs languishing on a shelf that no one has had the time or opportunity to make use of. You can be the first. Software allows even very young students to write stories and create background illustrations. Those teachers who have Internet connections can visit Web sites that have hundreds of pictures to download for free or Web sites that publish student writing. There are even Web sites to help you build your own classroom Web sites or print a classroom newspaper online.

In this section, information is provided regarding specific software programs, and summaries are given about Internet Web sites that may be helpful to your students.

The information is shared as a starting place for your journey of discovery as you explore the tools available to help enhance your publishing experiences with students. Please remember, information regarding computer software, as well as the validity of Internet Web sites, changes quickly. Some sites truly are here today and gone tomorrow. Keep in mind, if a particular site is no longer available, a similar site may be found by typing in key words to begin your search. For additional information, type in one of the following phrases as key words:

- Free educational clip art
- Online publishing for students
- Creating an online newspaper
- Desktop publishing for kids
- Building a classroom Web site

In most cases, you will see a list appear of many Web sites that fit the criteria of your key words. If you do not have the time to explore the sites yourself, ask a parent or volunteer who enjoys working with technology to explore some sites for you and give input about the sites you may want to explore further. Some sites charge a small fee for participation. Others have no cost. Always read the information about a site that explains the purpose of the site. That way, you can be sure the site is appropriate for your students to visit, and you can be relatively certain parents should have no concerns. Also, read the privacy statement and terms of publication before submitting student writing to be published on an Internet site. Don't let all of this information deter you. Just take the time to read the details printed on-line before embarking on an Internet adventure at any Web site.

Free Educational Clip Art

Clip art is the term given to all of those wonderful illustrations that students can use to illustrate writing. Many school supply stores carry books of printed clip art drawings that can be enlarged or reduced, colored, cut, and pasted to student writing. Most word processing software programs include small clip art libraries. Many publishing software programs include large selections of clip art. Now, literally hundreds of drawings, as well as color photographs, can be printed from the Internet, as well. Even if students are not ready to type their writing into the computer, they can enjoy searching through clip art libraries, and printing off just the right illustrations to accompany their writing projects. Most sites include sections about Terms of Use and Copyright Information. Please read these sections before printing. The following sites offer free clip art for printing or for importing to another Web site:

- **Classroom Clipart** (www.classroomclipart.com) includes over 30,000 free clip art images. Categories include, but are not limited to, animals, dinosaurs, foods, geography, habitats, nature, people, plants, science, space, sports, transportation, and weather.

- **Awesome Clipart for Kids** (www.awesomeclipartforkids.com) is part of a K-12 educational site, EduHound.com. Clip art categories are divided into General and Holidays.

- **Discovery Channel School's Clip Art Gallery** (http://school.discovery.com) Categories include art, health and safety, letters and numbers, math, music, science, social studies, and technology.

- **Teachnet** (www.teachnet.com) Categories include animals, food, holidays and seasons, school, and recreation. Each image is available in a printable black and white form, as well as in a coloring sheet size. Images can also be saved and imported into other programs.

Publishing Software

Software is all around us! It is available in computer stores, electronics stores, discount stores, and even at some grocery stores! How in the world do you choose? Never buy anything you haven't researched. Be sure you know what the program does, the grade level(s) it serves, and the type of computer and basic system requirements needed in order to run it effectively. It would be best for you to see the program in operation in order to determine the level of difficulty of maneuvering through the program components. Does it meet the needs of your students in a user-friendly manner, or must you have an advanced understanding in the way computers work in order to figure out how to manipulate the program? Remember, you are probably going to be the one who is the "expert" in the classroom. You want to be prepared.

The good news is, many software companies now realize the necessity of developing software that is easy to use the first time. Many programs have tutorials to train the new learner. Most also have "Help" menus to access when you get into a tight spot. Some programs also still come with good old printed manuals and/or toll-free numbers to call for technical assistance.

Software can be purchased to fit your circumstances. Individual packages suit the class with one computer. Some companies adjust the pricing when programs are sold in sets of 5, 10, etc.

Many software programs can be purchased in lab packs to accommodate a large number of computers. Schools can sometimes purchase a "site license" which allows a specific number of computers to access the program on a networked system. If you have a computer coordinator in your district, she can offer advice regarding the specific requirements appropriate to your school's situation.

Finding Affordable Publishing Software

- Apply a portion of your allocated classroom funds.
- Research the use of a specific program, then write a short proposal to present to a local civic organization, asking for funding and explaining how you would incorporate the use of the program into your teaching for the benefit of students.
- Make use of your share of funds from a school moneymaking project.
- Depending on price, suggest the software as a donation from parents to the classroom publishing center.

The following programs are just a few of the myriad publishing programs that exist. Learn more about any of the programs by typing the Web addresses in your Internet browser or calling the listed toll-free numbers.

- **SuperPrint Deluxe** by Broderbund, Tom Snyder Productions, A Scholastic Company (www.tomsnyder.com) for grades K-6. Students can create text with available graphics or can include their own artwork. The program includes 11 special fonts and patterns. 1-800-342-0236

- **Ultimate Writing and Creativity Center** by Riverdeep (www.riverdeep.net) for elementary grades. Students can write reports, newsletters, or stories. They can create signs and write in journals. Students can access a large graphics library. The program also gives students the capability of incorporating sounds into their writing. There are 1,000 writing projects and story starters to get students writing! Students can even hear their writing read back to them if the computer they are using has a microphone. 1-800-242-6747

- **Kid Pix Deluxe 4 for Schools** by Riverdeep (www.riverdeep.net) for grades K-8. With Kid Pix, students of all ages can combine text and graphics to create projects. Teachers can create project patterns and add instructions for students. Students can access a large graphics library as they create interactive stories. There are "Getting Started" movies to help students understand how to operate the program. A Spanish language mode supports ESL learners. 1-888-242-6747

- **Sunbuddy Writer** by Sunburst (www.sunburst.com) for grades K-2. This is a picture and word processor designed with young writers in mind. Students can choose from a wide range of subjects included in the story starter component or choose their own topics. Rebus images can be added to the text. Students can record their stories and may add sound effects to the text. 1-800-321-7511

- **Easybook Deluxe** by Sunburst (www.sunburst.com) for grades 3-8. Students can write and illustrate reports and stories, then print their writing in book format. Books can be printed in four different sizes. Students can hear their stories read aloud with the text-to-speech component. Students may illustrate their work with hand-drawn, computer generated, or imported graphics. 1-800-321-7511

Sites for Student Publishing

There are many sites on the Internet that publish student writing. Some sites publish only one type of writing, such as poetry. Some sites accept writing pieces only from students in particular age ranges. There are sites that accept all submitted entries, for a fee, and sites that do not charge fees. Please be sure to inform parents about your intention to submit student writing for publication because most sites require some type of publishing permission information for each student submitting a piece of writing. Spend some time exploring a variety of sites to find the one that meets your needs before submitting students' writing.

- **Kids' Space** (www.kids-space.org) This site is extremely easy to use—very "teacher friendly." Click on the section "For Teachers" to find a step-by-step guide for submitting class stories. Stories are not edited and will be posted exactly as received. Ten submissions may be sent at one time. The goal of this site is to provide a space where people from "a wide variety of cultural backgrounds can communicate comfortably and peacefully."

- **Candlelight Stories** (www.candlelightstories.com) This site publishes illustrated storybooks, under a section called KidBooks, that have been mailed in for submission. Parents and teachers may request to receive a free newsletter. Students may read other on-line storybooks that have been submitted.

- **Kid Authors** (www.kidauthors.com) Students may submit stories and poems by typing their writing directly into the on-line submission form. Several teachers have sent in written statements that describe their positive feelings regarding their class's publishing experiences at the site.

- **Kidscribe** (www.kidscribe.net) This bilingual site accepts submissions of stories, poems, and jokes. Student information is filled out on-line, and a space is provided for typing the submission on-line.

- **KidPub** (www.kidpub.com) One section, KidPub Schools, is set up to receive class submissions. Class participation costs $25 per year. For this fee, your students receive "unlimited posting of stories, pictures, and other creative works for every child in your class on your class page, a free one-year membership in the KidPub Author's Club for each child, which allows them to post stories and participate in activities on KidPub outside your class page, complete control over which stories are posted, and a simple click-and-choose way to update your page and add or remove students."

Creating a Classroom Web Site

Imagine the excitement your students would feel if they could publish their writing on their own classroom Web site! Imagine the motivation they would feel to produce pieces to be published. Wouldn't it be great for families to access your classroom site on the Internet anytime they wish to see their children's published writing selections? Grandma would be so proud!

Many school districts have created Web sites each teacher can link to in order to share classroom information. Check to see what is available in your area.

There is a design language, HTML, that is used to create a Web site. However, software exists to guide you through the steps of creating a classroom Web site even if you have no knowledge of HTML. You may wish to learn more about Web Workshop Pro and Web Workshop 2.0 by Sunburst (www.sunburst.com). These programs allow students from second grade and above to create Web sites. Web sites can be designed and published in a single class period. Accompanying teacher materials make it easy for anyone to design a Web site.

Education World has quite an informative Web site about a variety of topics of concern to teachers (www.educationworld.com). One article describes the software their Tech Team has chosen as the best for creating and posting Web pages. These programs are developed for creation by adults but can be used by students. The software programs vary in price from free to $299. You may find a program that will work for you.

A few sites on the Internet offer to help you create your classroom Web site on-line, without utilizing the HTML computer language. Sites to consider include:

- **Scholastic** (www.scholastic.com) Click on Class Homepage Builder. You will see a tutorial to help guide you through the step-by-step process, as well as a place to register to create your Web page when you are ready.

- **Free Web Hosting** (http://members.freewbs.com) There are example sites to visit, testimonials from users, frequently asked questions, information about the services available, and the terms of use.

Celebrate Writing

Take advantage of every opportunity for students to share their writing. Create situations that encourage writers to share confidently and that teach students to listen respectfully. Share daily, weekly, monthly or yearly. Just share!

Whenever possible, let students choose the writing they wish to share. Create a file for each child at the beginning of the year. Compile a variety of writing samples for each child during the year. Be sure to mark the date each piece was written. At the end of the year, you will have a good selection of pieces for each child to share at your end-of-year writing celebration. The writing pieces can also be used when holding parent conferences throughout the year as examples of student progress.

Suggested Activities:

- **Authors' Spotlight**: Designate a specific area in your room where volunteers come to share their writing with the other members of the class. Cut a large yellow circle out of poster board or construction paper to represent a spotlight. Attach the circle to the chalkboard, wall, or some permanent structure in the designated area. Display the lettering *Authors' Spotlight* around the top edge of the circle.

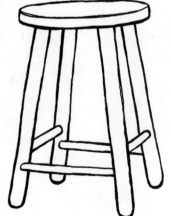

- Explain that the student "in the spotlight" is there to share her writing. It is time for everyone else to be quiet and respectful while the author is sharing. Afterwards, students may comment or ask questions about the writing they have heard. To help students verbalize comments or questions, write these sentence starters on the board or on a chart near the Authors' Spotlight.
  - I like the part _____
  - I want to know more about _____
  - I didn't understand the part _____

- **Writers' Rendezvous**: Once a month, spend the last hour of the school day sharing writing. Pair students or create small groups. Have students choose pieces of writing they have completed to share. Let students find a cozy corner of the class or go outside if weather permits. Give each student time to share his writing and have the other students in the group comment or ask questions in a positive manner. Circulate among the pairs or groups of students so that you can hear a little of everyone's writing!

- **Calling All Authors**: Sometimes, students get tired of sharing only with the other members of the class. Create a larger audience! Get together with the other classes in your grade level. Have each student choose one or two writing pieces to share. Be sure students' names are on each piece for easy identification. Meet with the other classes in the media center, cafeteria, or any large area in your school. Display writing pieces on tables. Allow students to browse, choosing one piece at a time to read. Set aside some time for students to share their writing aloud.

- **Authors' Tea**: Hold an Authors' Tea in your classroom. Send invitations home to invite families and other interested people to come to hear students share their favorite pieces of writing. Make copies of the invitations patterns (pages 71-73) and let students fill them out and deliver them. Perhaps your tea could be held in conjunction with an open house at your school. Make it a big deal! Encourage students to dress in their best. Let students make cookies or finger sandwiches in class to serve at the tea. Be sure to invite the school principal! (Before completing any food activity, ask parental permission and inquire about students' food allergies and religious or other preferences.)

- **Writers' Fair**: Hold a school-wide event. Invite all classes in the school to participate. Your fair might be held in conjunction with the end-of-the-year parent/teacher meeting or in conjunction with a book fair. Have each class set up a booth or decorate a table in the cafeteria, gym, or media center. Display student writing for all to read. Place flyers around the school to advertise your Writers' Fair. (See the flyer template on page 118.) Invite members of the school board and town governing bodies to come to see one of the good things happening at your school!

Come to our Writers' Fair

Date: _____

Time: _____

Place: _____

Come and enjoy original works by our talented authors!

Classroom Publishing Toolbox • CD-104098 • © Carson-Dellosa

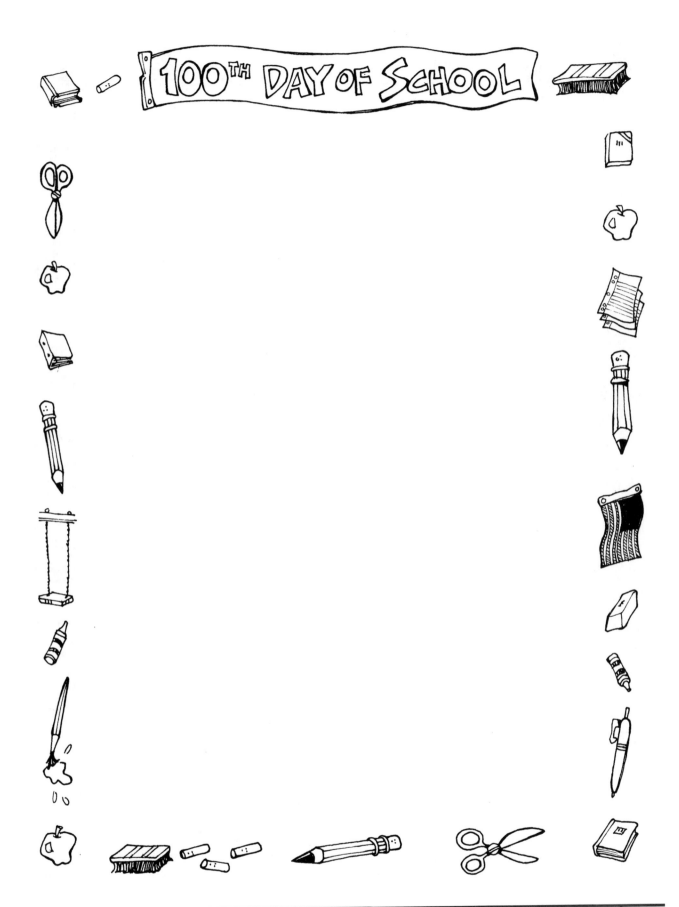

100ᵀᴴ DAY OF SCHOOL

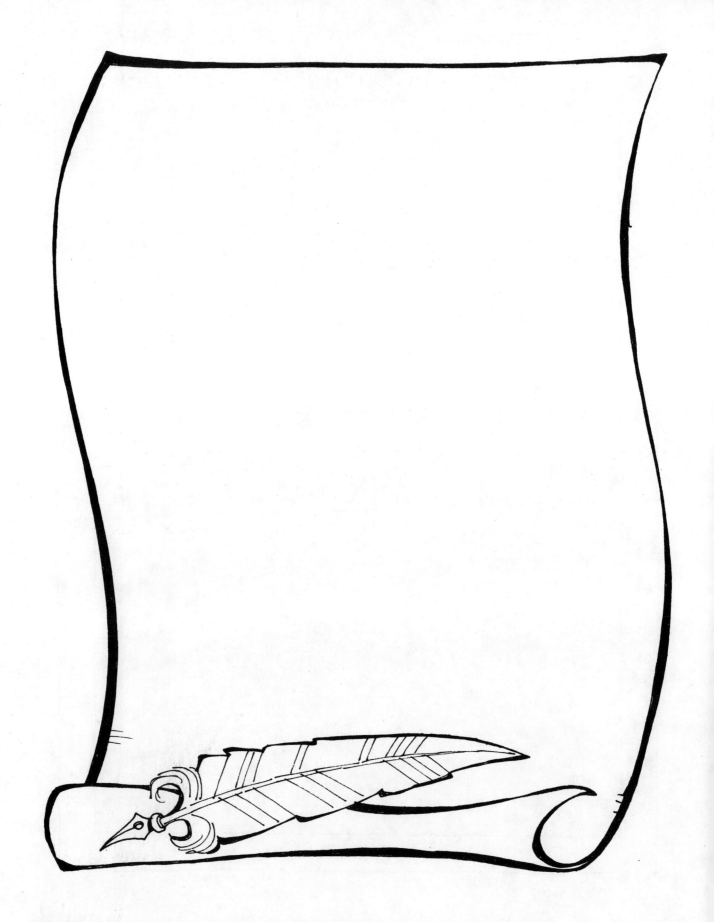